The Shyness
And Social Anxiety Workbook
For Teens

How to Recognize and Improve
Anxiety States, Relationships, Fears in Adolescents
with Practical Tips and Guided easy and Fun Exercises

By

Tracy Frank

Table of Contents

INTRODUCTION

As a teen, Joy was struggling with shyness and social anxiety. Social situations made her feel intense self-consciousness and fear of rejection that led to a range of negative feelings, including embarrassment, annoyance, anger at herself or others, low self-esteem, and depression.

Joy's parents noticed these changes in their daughter but had difficulty understanding what was happening. They invited Joy to join an adolescent mental health workgroup at the hospital, where they worked as part of a research study to help teens with mental health symptoms.

"Sometimes I'll start talking in class," she said in a meeting with her therapist and the study team members, "and I'll catch myself not making any sound. I feel like a total dork, and I can hear everyone laughing or looking at me, and then I just freeze. I'll look for somewhere to hide and then start worrying about that. I joke with my friends when the bell rings, but inside I feel pretty awful.

These feelings were triggered by social situations, which made her anxious and gave her opportunities to examine things that she didn't like about herself. Shyness and social anxiety are often symptoms of a more general problem in adolescence, which goes back to the teen years.

Despite the prevalence of mental health problems in youth and a lack of research on adolescent mental health in treating and preventing adolescent anxiety disorders, there is little understanding of how to intervene effectively in this stage of development.

It is difficult to identify and characterize early symptoms such as shyness or social anxiety precisely enough for effective treatment or prevention.

A survey by the World Health Organization for the United Nations (WHO/UNICEF) in 2009 determined that almost a third of all adolescents reported feeling shy or embarrassed often, or often enough, to interfere with their daily lives.

The development of social anxiety disorder (SAD) begins in childhood as an inhibited and anxious feeling in situations that are important or enjoyable for a child. In contrast, children with social phobia have an exaggerated and persistent fear of being judged negatively by others about themselves or the situation.

The intensity of the feelings can vary from mild to severe, causing embarrassment, blushing, trembling, sweating, shaking hands, and even a loss of voice during speech. Children may avoid social situations to avoid embarrassment.

Over time, they may stop participating in activities they enjoy and lose friends.

The cycle of avoidance and embarrassment in adolescents with social anxiety disorder can lead to more severe symptoms and consequences related to school, family relationships, or peers.

In addition, 11% of adolescents with social anxiety disorder report depression as a problem.

SAD is also linked to other psychiatric disorders, including bipolar disorder or schizophrenia; about 1 in 3 children with SAD has some other form of mental illness (e.g., attention deficit hyperactivity disorder or major depression).

Do you fear someone might look at you and think badly of you? How about being teased or laughed at by your friends? Do you feel anxious when you hear the school bell ring? If so, you may be struggling with social anxiety.

The following information can help explain why some people feel awkward in social situations and how certain feelings affect their daily lives.

At the heart of shyness is an intense desire for closeness. When we feel shy, we're often afraid of how others will react to us, even though we aren't sure what will happen. Our fears are often unfounded but still keep us from connecting with others.

We avoid people and situations because we fear how their reactions affect us. At its worst, a social anxiety disorder can make a person lose the ability to make friends, keep friends, or go out. It can cause the teen to spend more time alone, further isolating them from others.

Social anxiety can make being around other people so stressful that it overwhelms them, and they may try to avoid being around others altogether. A shy person can become a teen with a social anxiety disorder if they continue to avoid social situations, and that avoidance continues over time. Avoidance is the root of the problem. It keeps us from getting the feedback we need to understand how others see us, whether they judge us negatively or positively.

Avoiding new situations also prevents us from building coping skills and learning to control our fears. We don't get better at handling social conditions—the fear becomes more robust over time and can spread to other areas of our lives.

People with social anxiety disorder typically begin having symptoms in adolescence, when the desire for more independence and self-definition becomes strong.

This book presents a model for understanding shyness and social anxiety during adolescence. I use the movement into young adulthood as a point of transition, a time when social pressure is likely to become more severe. Most adolescents go through periods of shyness and other awkward behaviors, marked by periods of not caring what others think or trying too hard to fit in.

Adolescents who seem confident may be secretly anxious about how they'll look or what they'll say and find others' attention off-putting. Some teens want to be popular but aren't sure how to express themselves; others wish to be friends but aren't sure how to get close to people comfortably.

I have dealt with adolescent shyness and worked with adults with social anxiety difficulties. I believe many people feel uncomfortable and anxious in their first few high school years, physically and emotionally unprepared for all the changes and challenges they might face. It is difficult for most of us to know what is going on during the two to five years we are in this stage of development.

I have written about these issues because I hope that a better understanding will allow you, or your son or daughter, to be more effective in dealing with shyness or social anxiety or to recognize when your fears are out of control.

I am an authority because I have worked with thousands of young people who have social anxiety disorder and are facing the challenges of adolescence. I work with teenagers between 12 and 21, helping them to manage what tends to be an overwhelming period of social change. I believe that shyness, social anxiety disorder, and related disorders such as social phobia can be understood in our developmental transitions from childhood to adolescence and adolescence to young adulthood.

The language we use in talking about shyness or social anxiety helps us understand these disorders. As you'll see, this book includes the words "shy" and "fear," which describe feelings many people experience as they move into young adulthood.

I also use the word "anxiety," a common term used by clinicians and parents to describe mental states associated with different disorders.

One of the things that makes adolescence so tricky is that we are trying at the same time to adjust to several different levels of change, including physical changes (rapid growth spurts), emotional changes, intellectual changes (maturing thinking styles and interests), and social-emotional changes (the expectations of being liked or fitting into peer groups).

After reading this book, you will learn the biological and psychological reasons for shyness and the role that avoidance plays in causing social anxiety in young people.

You will learn about the many different types of social anxiety, how they are similar, and how they differ. You will also learn about common behavioral patterns that contribute to your feelings of shyness or social anxiety, such as avoiding new situations or making friends with other teens only when you're sure you have their full attention. You will learn about the powerful effect peer pressure can have on a shy teenager and how negative thoughts can keep us from getting the help we need.

Adolescence, the transition from child to youth

Adolescence is a time of tremendous change and growth. Between the ages of 13 and 18, young people experience physical, psychological, and social changes that affect their identity and their relationships with family members, teachers, friends, and peers. As children transition into adulthood, they tend to change their desires and values. They are more concerned with what others think to impress or gain attention and how they appear. It is a time of immense changes leading to inner and outer conflicts. There are distinct struggles for the transition from childhood through adolescence that come with being an adolescent. For example, many young adults who were shy growing up become even more reluctant and introverted when faced with social situations in adulthood.

The risk of developing social anxiety disorder increases during adolescence as young people become more aware of themselves concerning others. However, research shows that if someone has an anxiety disorder as a child or adolescent, there is usually no long-term adverse effect on their ability to function in later life. One of the struggles adolescence brings is shyness or social anxiety disorder, which affects about 15% of adolescents at one point during their lifetime. When shyness or social anxiety disorder affects an adolescent, it is referred to as social phobia or social anxiety disorder in children.

Children's social phobia or a social anxiety disorder can be seen very early in life. For instance, as infants, some babies will cry at the sound of a vacuum cleaner; that is an example of an infant showing fear of loud noises and the source of their worries. Outgrowing fears are usual, but if they continue beyond infancy and into childhood, they may be considered a problem(Fears).

It is important to note that other disorders can look similar to shyness but present differently and require different treatment methods. Any child or adolescent will feel some anxiety when the day begins and begin their first day of school. However, some children feel great stress when they do not know what is expected of them and how to carry themselves. This feeling can worsen as adolescents transition into adulthood, with many sense inadequate about themselves, afraid of being laughed at or ridiculed by others and hurting their feelings. The fear of being judged and feeling inadequate are fundamental to many, and they are afraid. This can cause the child or adolescent to isolate themselves, avoid making friends or participate in social functions. This is not malicious intent, simply a defense mechanism for young people who feel uncomfortable about themselves and do not want to be ridiculed by their peers.

Individuals with a social anxiety disorder also experience physical symptoms like nausea, upset stomach, headaches, hot flashes, sweating, and shaking in social situations. They may feel dizzy when facing group activities where they must get up and address the class. Others may experience anxiety before talking to someone new, feeling panicky and having trouble breathing. Others might feel chest pain, heart palpitations, and shortness of breath. Additional physical symptoms experienced by individuals with social anxiety include facial flushing, blushing, chest pain, or headaches during a social event.

Social Anxiety Disorder (SAD) is a mental health condition that causes an individual to fear social situations or interactions. It is important to note that not all shyness is seen as a mental condition. Shyness has been used as a defense against believing in their value as an individual. Still, many individuals have some form of low self-esteem.

It is a myth that shyness and social anxiety develop only as we grow older. For children and adolescents, shyness may not be as noticeable. However, this does not mean it cannot still be present. Shy people often experience more problems as they transition into adulthood because they have grown accustomed to a certain level of comfort in social settings. Therefore, it is essential to begin by teaching yourself the proper behaviors when you enter a challenging situation. Having self-control is the first step toward overcoming shyness.

Most people experience some level of shyness or social anxiety in childhood; however, the onset of social anxiety disorder is usually during adolescence or early adulthood. There are several negative consequences associated with excessive shyness and social anxiety; moreover, research shows that severe levels of shyness and social anxiety are strongly linked to perfectionism and behaviors such as drug abuse and self-injury. Cautiousness is an adaptive quality in some situations; however, for someone who experiences extreme anxiety about making mistakes or being humiliated in front of others, this quality can become a destructive pattern if left unaddressed.

Young people with social anxiety disorder suffer from a fear of being embarrassed, judged, or rejected by others. They develop a negative view of self and overestimate how others view them. At some point, as many as 20 percent of adolescents experience an anxiety disorder. Most teens with social anxiety disorder suffer in silence, thinking it is normal to feel nervous in certain situations. All too often, however, this shyness can lead to isolation and loneliness when young people avoid their peers because of their fears. As a result, they are missing out on the social skills they need to develop effective relationships and succeed in school and the workplace.

For you to get the most out of this workbook, you must be honest with yourself about whether or not you are shy. Once you have identified your level of shyness, read the sections that relate to your experience level. As you progress through the assignments in this book, if you find that some exercises are too demanding, take time to practice before moving on. If they are easy for you, challenge yourself and try other activities that seem more difficult initially. Whatever level of anxiety or fear you feel now will gradually be reduced due to working through the assignments in this book. In some cases, completing the exercises will take more than one attempt, but this is normal and only a sign that you are working through your anxiety. If you find some assignments too hard for you now, feel free to skip them if you wish.

When overcoming shyness or social anxiety, you mustn't let your symptoms become overwhelming or take over your life. This can lead to negative consequences such as depression and even suicide. Don't forget that there's always tomorrow! You may have this workbook for several weeks before completing all the exercises. Relax and take your time as long as you feel comfortable with what has been covered at the end of each section. When you begin any new task, the easiest thing to do is repeat some past action that was successful for you. However, what works for one situation may not work for another. For example, if you are shy about public speaking or talking to other people at school, it is important not to always rely on how well you performed before.

Anxiety is a normal part of adolescence, but if it occurs to the point where it begins to interfere with school or other important life tasks, it may be time to seek some professional help. Try practicing saying something in front of a mirror as often as you need. Soon enough, your voice will become stronger and more confident. If you are too nervous about appearing foolish in front of a group, try speaking out loud from the moment you wake up until the time your bed covers become too warm. This may feel awkward at first, but soon you will begin to get used to it.

Adolescence is a time for the emergence of all kinds of new and exciting ideas and personal growth. Unfortunately, this usually also means it is a time of awkwardness and self-consciousness. This chapter will help the reader understand the possible causes of social anxiety during childhood and adolescence, as well as how to overcome those fears and start to enjoy life again

The exercises in this chapter will help you pinpoint what's causing your social anxiety and learn how to cope with your situation.

As part of the normal process of growing up, you will need to confront many social situations in which others evaluate and judge your behavior. Social anxiety is common among adolescents. A 1997 study of teenagers in high school found that as many as 20 percent have symptoms of social anxiety. It's not that they are all afraid to talk to people. They are. But there is also a good chance that your child will experience social anxiety when called on in class, when speaking up in a meeting or group discussion, or even when being observed performing a task or work in school.

Social anxiety disorder is characterized by an intense fear of being watched and judged by others, causing the person extreme discomfort in social situations and distress out of proportion to the problem at hand.

Shyness, although a normal stage in personality development, can have negative consequences during this sensitive time because conflicts between "old" and "new" parts of the self can lead to anxiety or even depression. However, those who have reached their teens or twenties have the power to decide if their shyness will be an asset or a handicap for their future.

Many people grow up in shy and withdrawn situations and must hide their genuine emotions to be accepted. Shyness and social anxiety are very common in adolescence as many students begin to explore new social norms. At this time, students may feel uncertain about what is appropriate to say and do and how to make friends.

Many people are misinformed about shyness and social anxiety. Many people think being shy means being strange or crazy while being shy means being highly sensitive to criticism. Shy students can be very friendly, but they feel uncomfortable talking to people because they fear being ridiculed for minor mistakes or misfortunes. Social anxiety is a fear of humiliation that stems from the feeling that you will be judged by others and poorly evaluated. Most students with social phobia are confident in their academic skills, even if their social skills lack confidence. Many shy students were once outgoing until a negative experience made them afraid of new situations. Shyness and social anxiety can lead to many adverse outcomes, including poor grades, low confidence, trouble making friends, and difficulty with dating. If students can find ways to manage their fear, they will feel more confident, creative, and fully alive.

As an adolescent, you may feel shy about a few things. You may be afraid of sharing your likes or dislikes because of how people will react. Your fears come from not knowing the consequences of the actions you take. You want to fit in with the group, but at the same time, you don't want to be judged for your actions because sometimes people are critical of what others do. People often judge you for things that have nothing to do with you. They behave differently towards others just because they want attention or to make themselves look good in front of others.

In this situation, you want to be liked by your parents, your friends, or your boyfriends, but at the same time, you do not want to be judged because of the things you do. You may also dread people's stares and comments on your looks and even what they think of you.

But if you make a wrong choice, it can majorly impact everyone around you. For example, if most people are looking at your favorite book and saying it is boring, they will probably also say that reading is not fantastic. They will make fun of everyone who likes to read, which can create discomfort in many people who are embarrassed by accusations against them.

People will probably judge you if you do something stupid that doesn't turn out well, like falling or hurting yourself. Many students worry about what others think but don't realize that they choose to make their own choices based on their experiences. When you are worried about what others think, it's essential to realize that how you act is a choice and not the result of peer pressure.

Remember, people may not always be friendly, and even nice people can be mean sometimes when they feel someone has wronged them. Before worrying about what other people will think, try to listen to what they are saying and their tone. Most of the time, people do not know how to express their anger productively and just complain about the world around them. Asking questions about what others are saying can be a great way to get to know someone and see if you two share anything in common.

If you are shy or have social anxiety, even as an adolescent, you must begin to build your social skills by working on projects with others. You might be a perfectionist who worries about whether people will like them for any reason, which will affect the process. Even if you are shy or have social anxiety, taking risks and being honest in your actions is the most important thing. Taking risks may make mistakes, but this can help you learn from those mistakes and become stronger. This will make you more confident in your decisions and relationships with others. Over time, it may help you overcome shyness and build stronger relationships with friends and family members.

As an adolescent, try these steps to make your life a little easier.

1. Make an effort to talk to people about their interests, even if it is sometimes hard for you to do so. You don't have to join in the conversation

as that might scare you, but at least know what you can say next time someone brings up a similar topic.

2. Try to be helpful by offering to carry a bag or something similar or offering to help a person carry a box up an elevator or stairs. This simple action can impact someone's life, and you will be surprised at how they can reciprocate sometimes.

3. If you have nothing else to do, watch people as they do their business or sit in the cafeteria with your friends and talk about the people around you. You'll probably find that no one is paying attention to anyone else, so most of the time, people don't even notice other people, especially if they are not interested.

4. Try asking questions about things different from your own. You might

be surprised at the answers you'll get, but they will help you learn more about the world around you.

5. Read some books that will open your mind and teach you interesting things about life.

6. Talk to your teacher or counselor if you are having difficulty being friendly with others in class or within the school. Your teacher may find ways for you to succeed at talking to people and helping them achieve their goals.

7. If you have trouble talking with others, try to learn how to play an instrument or sport. This will help you break out of your shell and get used to being yourself on the outside.

8. Learn new things about how people talk and show them that you are

interested in learning more about their lives. If they don't know what to do next, tell them what they can do next, who they can talk to, or ask questions about.

9. If you cannot participate in a class discussion, ask questions about the subject matter and show that you are interested and willing to learn more about what is being discussed.

10. Try to talk to one person daily if that is all you can do. Remember, even just saying "hi" or "how are you?" can make someone's day, so don't worry if it doesn't come out perfect at first.

11. If your anxiety is so bad that you cannot speak with others without getting nervous, then practice talking to family members and other people who are not threatening and will be

supportive of your effort to speak out loud.

12. If you must speak, do so even if your voice shakes. People might laugh or make fun of you, but they will all secretly be delighted that you made an effort to talk to them.

Exercise 1: Differentiate Shyness From Social Anxiety Disorder

When you look out into the world, what percentage of the people you see do you think are shy? Do you look around and feel like almost everyone is shy or just that everyone feels uncomfortable in situations? If a person is having trouble answering this question, ask them to take a moment and consider their answer. Some people look at themselves and give themselves a higher number than they expect others to; however, answer honestly. The information corrects the false impression of how shy or socially anxious an individual is. Do you lose almost everyone

Boys may be more likely to respond that almost everyone is shy due to the boy's unwillingness to admit he has fears around other children. In this case, shyness is a defense mechanism for low self-esteem.

When you look at this exercise, what do you see?

Shyness and social anxiety disorder may be the same, but they are not the same. What is important to note in this exercise is that although shyness can be a defense mechanism, it is not seen as a mental illness or something that requires professional treatment. However, children with a social anxiety disorder will require treatment as they grow up and may need counseling or therapy to overcome their fear of social situations and to teach them how to interact with others.

Exercise 2

What would you do to help an individual with a social anxiety disorder who felt shy in a situation?

This second exercise is more tailored to helping an adolescent or child understand how they can help shy individuals.

An individual with a social anxiety disorder will often avoid getting up and speaking in front of others, but if they feel that they can handle it, they will seek a friend's help or treatment. They may also need reassurance that they are not alone in feeling how they do, which friends or family members can provide. Seeing how other people may feel and be anxious in social situations is helpful as individuals begin to recognize their fears and anxieties.

How to recognize anxiety states in adolescence

Anxiety isn't necessarily something that only happens to adults. Large-scale studies have shown that high anxiety levels emerge in childhood and may continue through adolescence and adulthood. This chapter will help you recognize the signs of one of these disorders affecting you. It will also offer strategies for helping you cope better with these problems, such as relaxation techniques, communication skills training, and assertiveness training.

Starting high school can be a stressful time for many teens. In this chapter, you will learn about your body's changes that may make you feel more anxious or self-conscious. Ascending from elementary to high school brings a new world of social experiences. You are bound to meet new people, try new things, and spend time in strange places with different rules than what you are used to. Social anxiety is an intense form of shyness. It is usual for children to experience varying amounts of shyness growing up. Shyness increases with age and may become more pronounced as the child gets closer to adolescence. Although many aspects of shyness can be dealt with and children can learn to overcome them, they can still feel the effects, including embarrassment in social situations or even fear of rejection by others. Social anxiety disorder is a condition with excessive fear or apprehension about being observed, evaluated, or scrutinized in social situations. This fearful avoidance of social interaction causes a child distress and often interferes with their ability to function normally in everyday life. Children suffering from social anxiety are more likely to avoid school, work, and other daily activities. They become overly self-conscious and insecure and may suffer panic symptoms if forced to speak in class or participate in group activities. They may worry excessively about making mistakes that embarrass them in front of their friends or peers. In an attempt to avoid the situations that make them feel anxious and fearful, children suffering from a social anxiety disorder often present with various physical symptoms such as headaches, stomachaches, nausea, and dizziness. The anxiety symptoms associated with social anxiety disorder typically develop during middle childhood through adolescence. It is not uncommon for children to have a phase of social anxiety that may last anywhere from a couple of months to several years in duration

You will learn to distinguish between normal social anxiety and an anxiety disorder. Most people experience a certain amount of anxiety when starting high school. But for some teens, the anxiety becomes so bad that it develops into an anxiety disorder. In this chapter, you will learn about the symptoms most likely to indicate a problem in your life. These symptoms may be signs of another form of mental illness: depression or an eating disorder like anorexia or bulimia. This chapter will teach you what types of things could be causing your symptoms. If your symptoms last over a few weeks, you must learn which factors could contribute to them. You can only overcome the problem once you know what's causing it. In most cases, certain factors are responsible for generating anxiety in teens. These include:

You will learn about the many kinds of anxiety disorders that may cause you to feel anxious or nervous in social situations. There are several types of anxiety disorders: panic attacks, phobias, generalized anxiety disorder, post-traumatic stress disorder, and obsessive-compulsive disorder. They all make social situations more stressful or uncomfortable than they need to be. You will also learn how to recognize common signs of depression in teenagers and how important it is to get help early if you think you may have this serious mental condition. More than one-third of teens will struggle with depression at some point.

Although this is often considered a mental health problem, it may also be connected to several other illnesses and disorders. If you have been diagnosed with an anxiety disorder, you must learn what could be causing your symptoms. If there is no physical reason for your symptoms—if they are not caused by something like an eating disorder, or if they come and go without cause—you will need to make sure that you get help as soon as possible.

While it is true that most people feel shy from time to time, social anxiety disorder differs from simple shyness; it is a severe mental illness that does not go away without treatment. In this chapter, you will learn about what social anxiety is and about its symptoms; reasons for why you have these symptoms (for example, genetic factors); and how to overcome social anxiety by changing your behavior and building self-confidence

How anxiety manifests itself in adolescence.

Cultivating the ability to live in harmony with the natural rhythms of our bodies and those around us—including animals, plants, and even the Earth—is much healthier than always trying to get more stuff or accumulate more possessions. Our bodies are made up of energy, known as our life force. When this energy is blocked and unable to flow freely through our body, it can cause various problems, including anxiety and stress.

Academic performance can be affected by both physical and social anxiety in adolescents. These exercises can help you understand why your social anxiety affects you and how you can improve. You can do the exercises each day or once a week at most. These are not meant to be exceptionally hard-hitting exercises. If the words seem to be working for you, go with them.

Some of the causes for this are:

- Increased concentration due to fear,
- Experiencing physiological symptoms of anxiety, such as being sick or shaken,
- Avoiding participation in classes and group discussions due to fear of judgment,
- Low self-esteem.

Anxiety disorders during adolescence might also be caused by certain life events, such as family problems or bullying. If anxiety is an on-going problem—not just a reaction to a particular situation—you must seek professional help. If you are experiencing social anxiety and are thinking about suicide due to your anxiety, get help immediately.

The adverse effects of social anxiety can be overwhelming, especially when they begin early in life. Social Anxiety Disorder can make it difficult for students to enjoy their free time and learn at school. Some of these adverse effects include:

- Feeling overwhelmed by the number of people watching and judging them,
- Feelings of inadequacy,
- Negative self-image,
- Loss of confidence as a result of feelings of humiliation and embarrassment.

There are times in life when we all feel sad, nervous, or stressed out. And while these feelings can be uncomfortable, they're also a normal part of living. Some of the signs that you may be dealing with an anxiety disorder are:

- Feeling anxious most of the time or having panic attacks,
- Not enjoying certain activities that used to be fun,
- Feeling depressed and hopeless about your future or the future of those around you.

You might suffer from a social anxiety disorder if you answered 'yes' to one or more of these questions. If this is the case for you, don't give up on your potential. You can do a lot to overcome social anxiety disorder and be the person you want to be. There are some common signs and symptoms displaying anxiety in adolescents. The most common symptoms displayed by an adolescent with anxiety include the following:

- Spraying of urine
- Bladder spasms

- Bowel spasm
- Abdominal pain, nausea, vomiting, and diarrhea
- Goose bumps, especially on the arms or legs
- Feeling lightheaded when standing up suddenly. This is because blood rushes away from the brain when standing up abruptly, which can result in falling if standing too quickly. Some people also experience a blackout, which can last for several seconds.
- Sweaty palms
- Tingling in the hands and feet, especially on one side of the body
- Trembling
- Sweating

The primary effect of anxiety in adolescents is that it could lead to them needing emergency health care, experiencing suicidal thoughts, or making suicide attempts. The leading cause is increased stress hormones in the body, which does not allow adolescents to control their emotions. Adolescents also have a high sense of responsibility which has been shown to make them more prone to depression and anxiety.

A traumatic experience does not necessarily cause anxiety. It can also be the result of feeling threatened, helpless, or in danger without being in any real danger. Most adolescents with anxiety experience symptoms at some point, and most will overcome it without treatment. Still, others will not be able to overcome it because they lack self-confidence and have strong negative beliefs about themselves and the outside world.

Overcoming anxiety at an early stage is vital so that adolescents can learn ways to avoid stressful situations that could trigger their symptoms in the future. Anxiety disorders are common in adolescence and can affect students' ability to learn, maintain relationships with peers, and complete academic tasks.

If anyone in the family suffers from anxiety disorders, it is crucial to be aware of this condition, as children may inherit a tendency to develop these disorders. The main thing that needs to be remembered is that recognizing these signs does not mean that an adolescent exhibits them all or suffers from a social anxiety disorder.

It is essential to look at the severity of the symptoms and how long they have been present to make a correct diagnosis.

Symptoms are usually more evident in adolescence, and this may be because individuals feel more vulnerable than adults do. As adolescents reach puberty, they become more self-aware and start to develop their own unique identities. This self-discovery process can be confusing and challenging, especially for shy adolescents.

Anxiety states in teenagers appear as follows:

Somatic symptoms- physical and emotional

Prolonged anxiety can lead to panic attacks, which are symptoms of panic disorder. Situations may also induce panic attacks that a person has never experienced before. Anxiety and fear can cause unexplained feelings of chest pains and choke. These feelings of discomfort are often called panic attacks. Mental health disorders in teenagers (anxiety disorders) are usually delayed by other physical or medical conditions or the teenager's behavior. This is because teenage moods and emotions may go unnoticed for some time, so that the onset can be unexpected for the teenager and his parents or doctors.

Behavioral symptoms- behavioral and emotional

The physical aspects can explain behavioral disorders (anxiety disorders) in teenage children discussed previously. Behavioral anxiety symptoms include avoidance of social situations, depression, irritability, poor concentration, and poor memory. Suicidal thoughts may also occur. The most common mental health condition in adolescents is depression (see depression in teenagers). Depression mainly affects teenagers because they are often unable to understand their emotions, and feeling of sadness is often misunderstood as being stupid or a sign that they can 'suck it up' and deal with their problems. On the other hand, depression can also be caused by environmental factors or family problems that are difficult to recognize or handle.

Cognitive and emotional symptoms-emotional

Teenage emotional anxiety symptoms include stress, isolation, crying spells, and loneliness. Some individuals with a social anxiety disorder may feel that others are hostile toward them. This is called paranoid delusion. It is common for adolescents with various disorders to have difficulty understanding their feelings and emotions. This is because, during adolescence, the individual's body is undergoing a variety of changes that include hormonal changes in the brain, which affect emotions; physically, they are going through puberty and may feel self-conscious about their body; socially, they are experimenting with relationships and groups. All these things make teenagers feel different from their peers, and they can trigger shyness or anxiety because of an overactive imagination or sensitive personality.

Cognitive and behavioral symptoms- cognitive

Anxiety can cause a person to be troubled. It often manifests itself through thoughts that are irrational and unhelpful. An individual may feel that something terrible will happen in the future or think they will make a fool of themselves in a social situation. These thoughts do not usually have any basis in reality but cause excessive worrying and confusion by exaggerating minor events. These kinds of fearful thoughts are called 'catastrophizing.'

Neurological symptoms- physical

Neurological symptoms include headaches, dizziness, trembling, and fatigue. There is often a feeling of numbness and tingling in the hands and feet; this is called paresthesia.

Do the following exercise to ascertain whether you have a social anxiety disorder. Next to each symptom, write "very rarely", "rarely", "sometimes", "often" or "very often". On the next page, enter the number of days in the last month you felt each symptom. Then select your scores from the table below.

Poor social skills - very rarely-1; rarely-2; sometimes-3; often-4; very often-5

Poor body image - very rarely-6 ; rarely-7 ; sometimes-8 ; often-9 ; very often-10

Be shy at social gatherings -very rarely: 1%; rarely: 3% ; sometimes: 10%; often: 20%; very often: 30%

Risky behavior -very rarely: 5%; rarely 10 %. Sometimes : 20% ,often :30% . very often: 40%

Insecure - very rarely: 2%; rarely: 5% ; sometimes: 10%; often: 15%; very often: 30%

Afraid of criticism - very rarely : 0% ; rarely : 1%. Sometimes :10%, Often: 20%, Very often : 30%.

School phobia - very rarely : 0% ; rarely: 2%; sometimes: 5%; often: 10%; very often : 20%

Hypervigilance - very rarely: 2%; rarely : 5% ; sometimes : 10%;often: 15%,very often: 25%

Avoiding social situations and conversations - very rarely :

4%, rarely: 10% ; sometimes : 20%, often :30%,very often: 40%

Regretting making mistakes-very rarely 3 %; rarely 10 %; Sometimes

20 % Often 30 % Very Often 40%.

Self-confidence: the score is taken by assessing the number of times you think, "I have a good social life." If you thought you had a 'good social life, mark "4". If you think, "I don't have a good social life," mark "0,"

or if you don't know, think about it for some time and select the answer that comes closest to your thoughts

Fears of being judged

Fear of being judged is not a common anxiety disorder among teens. However, it can cause many concerns in teenagers with social anxiety disorder. In some cases, teenagers think that they will be judged on their looks or size. Teenagers may also have irrational fears that they will not be as good at something as their peers. Being self-conscious is natural in teenagers; they often do not notice it.

On the one hand, they feel that they are too sensitive and experience fear when other people address them directly. They may become fearful that they are being ignored. Some teenagers with social anxiety disorder tend to over think their actions and speech, fearing that it will be ridiculed or refused. For example, a teenager afraid of being judged might fear speaking in public, looking at others directly, or standing near someone they do not know. On the other hand, they are afraid to make mistakes because this is regarded as a sign of weakness or ignorance. Teens need to know that many people would like to talk to them, and social anxiety disorder has nothing to do with being shy but with how you act when you are in front of people.

The most common way to overcome social anxiety disorder is to break social situations into small steps. This is because people commonly have difficulty handling change. A good example is learning a new sport or subject at school or college. If a person suddenly tried playing football, they would probably experience some anxiety until they got used to using different muscles and the action of slamming their head against another person's head after falling. However, trying out these sports requires kids to have the courage and confidence to try them out first.

Once an individual has enough confidence to overcome the fear of being judged, they will be less worried about making mistakes or embarrassing themselves in front of others. This will lead to more confidence in social situations. Teenagers with social anxiety disorder are always aware of how they look, and they can be reluctant to try out new activities because they might feel that others would strangely look at them if they failed. This, unfortunately, adds to the fear that the teenager is a failure and makes it even harder for them to become confident and make decisions for themselves. Encouraging teenagers to try out new activities and develop their personalities is one way to help them deal with social anxiety disorder.

Most teenagers fear that if they make friends with someone who then rejects them, this would be a sign of them being bad in some way. This can cause them great distress and lead to an increase in their social anxiety disorder. Teenagers are very conscious about what others think of them. In stressful situations, people often tend to blame themselves for things that have happened and feel isolated because they believe that no one else feels the way they do. Sometimes their perception is not realistic, and they are very popular. However, it can be difficult to know the truth, leading to teenagers feeling isolated in social situations.

Fear of being rejected or abandoned causes teenagers to withdraw from other people. They tend to wallow in self-pity and make themselves uncomfortable by creating situations in which they don't have to face other people. They often believe they are not good enough, and their social anxiety disorder is why. Teenagers need to realize that there is such a thing as a group of friends and that it is perfectly normal for a person to start with a small group of friends before expanding their circle of friends.

A great way of ensuring teenagers have more confidence in social situations is for parents to discuss any fears their children might have. This can help to reduce the fear of being rejected or judged and make teenagers less anxious about making friends. Parents can help their children to start a new hobby like going to the park, playing games with other kids, or joining a sports team at school. This will allow them to meet more people and be exposed to different situations that might make them nervous in the past.

Anxiety disorders in adolescents will often be coupled with fears related to being judged by others, being laughed at, and losing control or embarrassing themselves in front of others. For instance, one girl constantly worries that her friends will discover how "ditzy" she feels. She sees the faces of everyone around her in school, hoping they don't think she is stupid.

Over time, she has developed a behavior pattern that results in more anxiety as it becomes harder for her to hide how "different" she feels from others. This causes her to feel more and more anxious about doing things that used to be a pleasure.

"I am worried about my friends looking at me and thinking I'm weird."

The look on her face tells the story. Frightened, nervous, and trying not to show it. This is the look of someone who knows something is wrong with their life but doesn't know what it is.

She knows how much she wants to fit in and how badly she wants her friends to like her, but she also knows that something is getting in the way of that. What makes this situation so difficult is that she has no idea why this is happening or even what it feels like most of the time. She knows that things go wrong when she tries to act or speak in a way that will help her fit in. Her mind becomes blank. She can't think of anything to say. People look at her as though they are judging her and finding her wanting.

This is the kind of situation that can drive a person crazy over time. Those thoughts make it seem like something is wrong with her, making her feel even more anxious about being around people. If you find yourself in this situation, you must seek professional help. If you are experiencing social anxiety and are thinking about suicide due to your anxiety, get help immediately.

Social Anxiety Disorder (SAD) can make it difficult for students to enjoy their free time and learn at school. The world becomes a much more frightening place when you are socially anxious. The worry, fear, and self-doubt can affect your ability to concentrate on anything other than yourself.

This leads to the following:

- Poor school performance,

- Decreased interest in pleasurable activities such as sports or music,

- Problems with relationships.

When they can't avoid those situations, they try to appear perfect so that others will like them instead of trying to perform as well as they can, believing it doesn't matter. Another way students with social anxiety experience difficulties at school is by not being able to concentrate during class due to feelings of shame and embarrassment. This can make it difficult for them to concentrate and succeed in school.

The fear of being ridiculed or judged can significantly impact children's ability to learn and perform well academically. After suffering from a panic attack, some people may feel embarrassed about having one. However, panic attacks are not uncommon. Some studies also point to the fact that shy children finish school with lower grades than their non-shy counterparts. When they can't avoid those situations, they try to appear perfect so that others will like them instead of trying to perform as well as they can, believing it doesn't matter.

The following exercises are great ways to get yourself to overcome the fear of being judged by others.

Be aware that you are self-conscious. Write down your thoughts and feelings about yourself, what other people think of you, or what they might say to your face or behind your back. List all these fears on a piece of paper (ex: "I am too small," "I am not smart enough," "I am ugly," etc.)

Observe yourself in front of a mirror and write down what you are thinking about yourself (ex: "What does my nose look like?", "does I look fat?").

Next, find out how close friends feel about you and how outgoing they are in social situations. Some teenagers might think their friends don't like them, but this is not true. They might just be too shy to talk to each other.

When you think about social situations at school and college, ask yourself whether you would like to participate or not. Involve yourself in some activities you would like to do, but don't rush into them all the time! Find your limits in a social environment and try things out one step at a time. If something goes wrong, be prepared to move on to another activity that suits you better. This will help you overcome the fear of being judged by others.

Write down the things that you enjoy and find interesting about yourself.

Look for new things all the time. Try to discover something new, whether a sport, a sport, a hobby, or an after-school activity.

If you are afraid of being judged, try others' reactions to you in social situations; do they like you or not? If they do like you, what makes them happy? Can they help you overcome your fears?

Ask close friends to describe their fears of social situations. Some examples are: "What made me shy?", "What if I make a mistake?", "How far should I go?" etc.

If you find out that other people judge you negatively in front of others, do they tell you that they don't like you? Or do they simply tell you not to worry about it? Don't let their judgments affect your feelings if these are the answers. Instead of feeling bad about yourself, ask them what they feel and what they think.

Teenagers with social anxiety disorder need to hear that they make a difference in the world. They need to realize that their opinions are important because even if others do not like them or their actions, they will make no difference to them. Their peers pay attention to what is happening in the world and might even try and change things for the better

How much does genetics affect whether there is a tendency for anxious behavior in parents

Genetics studies how our traits and illnesses are inherited from our parents; the different combinations of genes within our chromosomes determine how we look. Genes also affect many other things about us, including the personalities and ways we behave. Scientists have found that certain genes can be passed on to children to make them more likely to develop certain conditions, such as social anxiety disorder or OCD.

This is because social anxiety disorder is regarded as a biological problem. People with this condition experience fear when they are in front of others, constantly think about themselves, and worry about being judged by others or embarrassing themselves in front of others. Those who experience social anxiety disorder have parents who may tend to it. However, this does not necessarily mean that all of their children will also be. On the other hand, some children have parents who suffer from shyness and social anxiety disorder, but their own is not. Many researchers consider the genetics of this illness to be unclear. On the one hand, there is evidence suggesting a genetic contribution to this disease; on the other hand, it can be argued that various other factors, like stress, cause social anxiety disorder, and genetics can also play a significant role.

Research has shown that families with social anxiety disorder are more likely to be at high levels of stress and self-esteem issues. This can also contribute to family members tending to experience a social anxiety disorder. Children with both parents suffering from this type of illness can learn techniques to help them develop the necessary skills to manage their anxiety. They can help their children manage these people's negative effects on their lives. These children may even have a better chance of overcoming social anxiety disorder since they can get different types of help and advice regarding managing their issues.

Both depression and Anxiety are genetic disorders. A person who tends to be socially anxious is more likely to develop a social anxiety disorder.

Children of anxious parents are more likely to develop social anxiety.

Anxiety and depression are genetic illnesses, and most people with these conditions were born with them, even though their parents may not know about them. For example, if the person has a parent with clinical depression, the risk of developing clinical depression is 50%. This means that if you have a parent who was diagnosed as having clinical depression, then you are 50% more likely to experience clinical depression than your friend whose parents never experienced it. After we age, on average, 1-2 years every year, we begin to think and act in a specific way, eventually leading to clinical depression. If a person's parent or close relatives experienced clinical depression, then the possibility of developing clinical depression goes up by 50%. The child tends to imitate their parents as he grows up. Therefore, if the parent has clinical depression, a child is more likely to have clinical depression. The child is unaware of this condition, and they cannot tell anyone about it, though it's seen in the eyes and behaviors of that person.

Some people are predisposed to anxiety disorder, although they never recognize it. These individuals may be diagnosed with an anxiety disorder later in life when they become more mature and begin to understand their personal history better. Their anxieties may develop gradually with no immediate cause for alarm or extreme stress. These anxious individuals may not be aware of this early childhood anxiety.

Genetics and Social Anxiety

A person's personality, behavior, attitudes, and skills are transmitted from generation to generation through genetics. It is also possible that a specific genetic variation may predispose an individual to develop a social anxiety disorder. Certain genes are linked to social anxiety in a way that does not lead to any clinical symptoms but does intensify the tendency for an individual to become anxious or even stressed in certain situations. Even though there is no medical test for predicting people who will be more prone to developing a social anxiety disorder, it can be considered when deciding whether you tend towards social anxiety. If you have a family member with this genetic variation, you must know when and how it can be triggered. Knowing what triggers the anxiety is essential for avoiding the onset of this condition.

Some people are aware of their tendency for social anxiety disorder when they fall into a panic attack or have to handle public speaking experiences. In this case, they have a trigger for their social anxiety in the form of an anxious event or situation that overwhelms them with fear and panic. Others may not know about these early signs of social anxiety but get better when making lifestyle adjustments to accommodate their condition.

The genetics that controls social anxiety have been identified and are being studied by scientists. Researchers have found a genetic link between social anxiety disorder and genes. Two dozen genes have been associated with anxiety in some way. This identifies the tendency that a person has to develop an anxiety disorder. Still, it does not mean they will become socially anxious because only a very small amount of people with this genetic predisposition develop an anxiety disorder.

Social Anxiety Disorder is one of many disorders known to be passed down genetically through families. Still, not everyone with an anxiety disorder has a family member who automatically has it. Sometimes, a person is unaware of the triggers for their social anxiety. This is why it is important to learn about your family history so that you can make changes for yourself so that the course of your life will not be affected. By knowing the different genes that can predispose you to social anxiety and your tendencies, you have a better shot at avoiding an anxiety disorder by taking action when you feel anxious. Your family members may not tell you about their condition, but they may begin to change their behavior once they see how serious the problem is. A person will realize that their anxiety disorder is not just a passing phase once they begin to see that it is affecting their life.

There is a connection between social anxiety and various personality traits. In particular, people with social anxiety have been found to have the following personality traits:

a. They are more likely to report higher levels of neuroticism than the general population,
b. They tend to have lower self-esteem as they are more likely to have a low sense of self-worth,
c. They tend to be perfectionistic and also fear negative evaluations by others.

The more you can relate to these personality characteristics, the better it will be for you. Those who are experiencing social anxiety disorder are not alone. The good news is that those who go through this struggle find help and hope. One way is using cognitive therapy for social anxiety disorder (COGTSA).

These three factors (physical health, social anxiety, and genetic makeup) can create a vicious cycle that results in ineffective treatment and poor school performance. A student may struggle in school and become more anxious about their performance even though they have never had any trouble with schoolwork. However, this cycle can be broken or reversed through effective treatment combined with an active approach toward learning in a controlled environment.

It is not only the fear that your children will be shy but also that they may develop other emotional problems, such as depression and substance abuse. It is hard for a parent to watch their child struggle with depression, especially if they know it could be due to genetics. The very nature of genes makes them difficult to avoid or escape. This can make it difficult for a parent to know how to act. But what can you do if you know your child may experience an anxiety disorder later in life? How can a parent participate in preventing social anxiety disorder if they don't fully understand how it works or how they can help their child? Various factors, including genetics, can cause social anxiety disorder. But there are steps that you can take to help your child with social anxiety disorder and other emotional problems.

If you know that your child and their social anxiety is genetic, there are some steps that you can take to help them out of this situation. However, according to research conducted by the U.S. National Library of Medicine (NLM), you must remember that social anxiety disorders are genetic. If they have a family history of depression or anxiety, they are more likely to have a similar response or reaction.

Yes, those diagnosed with a social anxiety disorder may need to attend therapy sessions, but it is also important that you don't push your child into therapy. Some believe that being in therapy will help them overcome their fear of loud environments and other situations. Still, it may lead them to a different type of anxiety disorder. Confrontation is not the only method for overcoming severe cases of social anxiety disorder. Another way is through cognitive behavioral therapies (CBT). The treatment that CBT offers has helped many people overcome their fear and anxiety in situations where they were previously unable to do so.

Social anxiety disorder should not be seen as a weakness; instead, it should be seen as a sign of strength. Those with social anxiety disorder can see their weaknesses and strengths in ways others cannot. A person with a social anxiety disorder has a strong sense of self-awareness that can be used to benefit the rest of the world. Many don't realize that those with social anxiety have a high level of creativity, intelligence, and sensitivity that can be used to create something positive and beautiful for the rest of the world.

Those who are experiencing social anxiety disorder are not alone. The good news is that those who go

through this struggle find help and
hope

Social network anxiety-addiction-cyber bullying

Social network sites have become an integral part of everyday life. In fact, on average, teens spend approximately 8 hours per day on these kinds of sites. They are some of the most popular and frequently used websites on the Internet today. Social Network Anxiety is also known as "SNA," It is becoming more common among younger generations as social media platforms have become popular in our society. It can be defined as a feeling of anxiety and insecurity on the internet that may cause social withdrawal and fear of being vulnerable in front of cameras due to the fear of being judged. It can also be a state of chronic fear that is caused by the fear of being judged or viewed negatively by people on social networks

This chapter will learn more about social network anxiety and how it affects people. Social networks are a great way of keeping in touch with friends and family, but they can also be a source of anxiety. Social network anxiety has been linked to addiction, the desire for negative opinions about oneself, and the intense need for approval from others. Recently, many people have been turning to these kinds of sites for help and support. Social network addiction is extremely similar to other types of addictions that people can develop toward things like drugs or alcohol. People who become addicted experience withdrawal symptoms typically when they have been deprived of using them for an extended period. Social network addicts may experience guilt from spending excessive time on these sites daily.

Social network anxiety can also be experienced when users receive negative comments and opinions from others. When this happens, many users repeatedly check their page to see what others say about them. They spend much time doing this instead of focusing on other aspects of their lives. The need for approval from others and the desire for recognition also play major roles in social network anxiety. When people receive only positive or negative comments from friends, they may start to focus on those things even more. This can cause them to develop certain forms of social network anxiety. Social network anxiety can also be developed through cyberstalking and online predators. This form of social network anxiety arises due to someone viewing an individual's status updates on a social networking site or having extensive access to personal information. This can lead to real-life consequences.

It is important for people experiencing this kind of anxiety to let their friends and family know they need help with this problem. They should also remove the people from their networks if they have not done so already. Keep in mind that people experiencing this form of anxiety typically do not feel comfortable opening up about it and may not want their friends and family to know about it. As a result, they may go to great lengths to hide the extent of their symptoms. They will often deny that they are exhibiting any negative or dangerous behavior. However, this is likely a sign of the problem. Social network anxiety is the most common form of social phobia. The disorder then falls under the category of specific phobia because the fears or anxiety are disproportionate to the situation.

Social anxiety disorder also has both personal and social limitations. The National Comorbidity Survey (NCS) found that as many as 13% of the population can be affected by a social anxiety disorder. However, only 30% ever seek treatment. There may be a lack of interest in seeking treatment because they feel that they are the only person with this problem, or they feel embarrassed or have a sense of shame. When it comes to seeking help for the reasons listed above, then there may be other possible issues, such as depression, substance use, or physical disabilities

Social network anxiety is an illness that causes people to start to feel anxious when using a social network. It can be caused by the person's social network or by an individual or even a group that is being discussed in the social network that they may not be familiar with. For example, someone may feel like an outsider if the people talking about them are those they don't know or have just met. However, some of the symptoms of this disorder can cause someone to question their entire life and self-worth. It is not just the people they meet or talk to on social networks but also those who use their pictures, post them, and then tag them.

Social network anxiety can occur when someone has an issue with their body, such as body dysmorphia, an eating disorder, muscular dystrophy, obesity, or even just a person commenting on how a picture makes them look. This can cause problems because it makes them feel they need to change their appearance. Another common symptom of social network anxiety is someone feeling like a cyber bully might be saying something negative about them, whether true or not. The fear of getting cyber bullied is one of the biggest issues for people with social network anxiety. When someone is talking about them or their picture, it can be easy to feel like they are being put down or humiliated. It can also cause the person to become socially isolated because they might start to avoid social situations. Some people may experience an anxiety attack at a social function, and their phone vibrates with a notification made on a social network.

The main factor behind this disorder is the person's anxiety and the judgment of others. Social network anxiety doesn't necessarily mean that the person will have panic attacks, but it does cause them to have a sense of upset and even depression. They might find themselves avoiding social situations or getting anxious when using a social network for as little as 30 minutes. In addition, many people don't have a social anxiety disorder but may have problems with cyber bullying and posting pictures or information that is disagreeable. This can cause someone to feel like they are being harassed or stalked, which is also a problem. Cyberbullying can be dealt with by going to the authorities or hiring a lawyer to sue the person.

Regarding social networks, this disorder has a lot of crossover with addiction. People tend to be more addicted to social media from around age 11–14 years old. This disorder is not just in groups but also in an individual. Those who suffer from social anxiety find that they cannot resist posting pictures to a network, even if this makes them feel uncomfortable. Some have social network addiction and spend an average of 10 hours daily on Facebook or Snapchat. By spending too much time on their phones, they do not get to interact with other people. Social network addiction is generally linked to problems such as depression and loneliness. The increased use of smartphones has decreased the amount of time that people spend interacting with others and having face-to-face contact; with the result being a decrease in real-life encounters

Selfies are pictures taken by a person with a smartphone or digital camera and shared with friends on social networks like Facebook and Instagram. The person taking the selfie posts them to their page or page group. Some people identify themselves with a certain group, and by doing so, they are putting themselves into a social situation where they may feel uncomfortable. The anxiety occurs because of some aspect of the situation that might differ from what they had previously experienced. People can feel like outsiders when someone new joins their group or their circle of friends changes. They may feel like they are excluded from festivities that were previously held in a social network. This feeling of being excluded is the root cause of why someone might get a social nervous disorder.

Social network anxiety can be classified as a social or psychological issue. As the name suggests, social network anxiety is typically caused by someone being too concerned about how others perceive them. When this concern causes you to spend excessive amounts of time worrying about what others think of you, it becomes clear that you have a social network anxiety disorder. Social network anxiety disorder is an extremely common form of anxiety that affects a large number of people each day. Studies show that almost nine out of every ten young people in the UK have some form of social media usage in their everyday life. Most of these users will suffer from social media anxiety at some point in their lives.

So, how can social networking and anxiety go hand in hand? For some people, social network anxiety is a real problem that can cause significant stress, discomfort, and distress levels. Thankfully, steps are taken to ease social media anxiety symptoms. In most cases, this kind of anxiety is very manageable in a healthy manner. However, suppose you are experiencing severe symptoms such as shaking or feeling like you need to breathe more quickly than normal. In that case, it may be time to seek professional help from a therapist specializing in managing mental health issues.

It can be difficult for people with social network anxiety disorder to overcome this problem independently. As a result, most people suffering from this kind of anxiety will benefit from external support to overcome these symptoms.

Social network anxiety disorder is typically found in young adults who regularly use the internet and social networking sites. Because social media and online platforms are extremely popular forms of communication these days, you may be more likely than ever to experience some form of social network anxiety. Also, due to the extensive nature of social media and online platforms, it becomes necessary for everyone to think about how they should act to keep themselves safe. While no one wants to experience negative incidents such as bullying or cyberbullying, which can be quite common on sites like Facebook or Twitter, it can make people feel uneasy when they leave the house.

Many people suffering from social network anxiety disorder feel they have two different emotions simultaneously. When this happens, it can feel like a constant state of extreme confusion. This is because people with social network anxiety disorder feel as though they are experiencing both anxiety and depression at the same time. In addition to feeling extreme levels of worry and distress, many people with a social network anxiety disorder may experience strong feelings of shame after each negative incident. This is known as secondary trauma.

These symptoms may surface after a series of negative incidents on or around one's social media profile. When this kind of anxiety affects a person's daily life, it becomes necessary to speak with someone who understands what you are going through. This can be a very difficult thing to do. However, people suffering from social network anxiety disorder must receive the support they need because they may not have anyone else available to help them at this time. While these feelings are quite powerful and may cause severe distress, they are not the only symptoms experienced by those with social network anxiety disorder.

One of the key symptoms associated with a social network anxiety disorder is known as social withdrawal. This anxiety can cause people to withdraw from showering public approval on their friends and connections on various online platforms. In most cases, a person suffering from social network anxiety will experience an intense fear of being perceived negatively by people around them. In other cases, individuals may accept that people may inflict significant harm upon them in response to their posting activity. Because many users are unaware of how others view these posts, they can be an extremely powerful source for individuals suffering from this issue.

Social network anxiety disorder can be quite difficult for the people who experience it because they feel that other people are constantly judging them. Unfortunately, this is not typically the case. While cyberbullies and trolls lurk around on social media sites, most people don't think about how others will perceive their social media posts. Many anti-social individuals might enjoy seeing how other people respond to online activities. One of the most common symptoms associated with social network anxiety may include feeling isolated and lonely even though your family or friends in person may surround you. While it is true that social media sites are great ways to keep in touch with family members and friends, they can also cause people to feel a sense of loneliness. This is particularly true when people use these sites excessively without realizing how much time they spend on them. Everyone needs to determine their limits and boundaries when using social media platforms to avoid feeling this anxiety.

Another common symptom associated with fear occurs when people begin to feel that any type of negative incident will automatically be posted online for the entire world to see. When this happens, people can begin to feel as though their personal and private information will be exposed for everyone to see. In other cases, it can cause people to believe others will expose their whereabouts. Some people may believe that the police are monitoring them. While these issues are certainly not good, they are not the only problems that can occur while suffering from a social network anxiety disorder.

When this kind of anxiety begins to manifest itself in a person's life, they need immediate help due to the intense symptoms that could result in a negative way or simply being ignored by others. In most cases, people with a social network anxiety disorder may not be aware that they are suffering from some form of social anxiety. However, once a person begins to recognize the symptoms that they are experiencing, they must seek help as soon as possible. While this may be difficult for many people, it can be extremely important for their general well-being and growth as an individual. Social anxiety can often be confusing to those who are not familiar with its symptoms and triggers. However, some telltale signs usually indicate a person is suffering from a severe social anxiety disorder.

If you have social network anxiety, you can try out these activities to help you manage your anxiety.

First, consider removing the people who you feel are a negative influence on your life. Avoid visiting your page frequently if it starts to hurt you. You may even want to consider deleting it if you have issues with it. You can also block and report any inappropriate comments or pictures that may be posted on your social network page as well.

Social Network Anxiety can harm one's life, mental health, and well-being. It is important to note that social network anxiety can be managed without any outside help and support. However, this may not always be the case. If social network anxiety is causing a significant amount of stress and discomfort, it is recommended that you speak with someone before this becomes a bigger problem for you.

Second, start up a blog or website of your own and get your creative juices flowing. You can publish your blog and relate it to what you are going through.

Lastly, you need to monitor how much time you spend on social network sites each day. Limiting yourself to no more than two hours per day would be best. If you spend more time online than this, you may consider finding alternative ways to spend your free time that do not involve social networking sites.

How to improve self-esteem in adolescents

Self-esteem is the concept that how we feel about ourselves is based on how others view us. People with high self-esteem are not threatened by negative feedback and can take it in stride. People with a low sense of self-esteem tend to be sensitive to negative feedback and may try to hide their low feelings to avoid people's disapproval. Adolescents generally tend to have higher self-esteem than adults because they believe they are still developing and thus have room to improve their behavior.

People with low self-esteem often tend to be more anxious than people with high self-esteem. Anxiety is a symptom of low self-esteem, and people with low self-esteem are more likely to seek counseling for anxiety or depression when it arises. People who suffer from anxiety can become so overwhelmed that they begin to shut themselves off from others. Self-esteem plays an important role in helping your social anxiety disorder and panic attacks are common symptoms of a specific type of phobia. The difference is that people with a social anxiety disorder also tend to fear negative evaluation by others. When a person has this type of phobia, all aspects of social interaction may be affected, including the way that person dresses and behaves in any given situation. It can affect almost every aspect of the individual's life, from their career to how friends and family interact with each other. The main focus of this book is a generalized social anxiety disorder, but this disorder can often be mistaken for other disorders. To treat the underlying problem, it is important to understand what causes it first and then attempt to treat it accordingly.

The most common cause of low self-esteem is anxiety. It may be due to social anxiety, depression, anorexia, or more serious problems such as abuse or neglect. It is important to remember that people with low self-esteem are likelier to fail in their goals and not achieve what they want. People with low self-esteem are less motivated, so they are likely to spend more time alone and not have friends or participate in activities. This type of behavior creates a cycle of negative thoughts, which creates a larger problem for someone who suffers from anxiety or depression.

These factors can also cause one's self-esteem to fall even lower, which just causes more problems for the individual who suffers from anxiety or depression. The problem with low self-esteem is that it can be very difficult to change. Many times, these feelings are a symptom of something else. Anorexia, for example, can cause anxiety and depression because the individual feels food is responsible for their problems. Suppose the individual receives treatment for their illness. In that case, they will probably need to improve their self-esteem to take good care of themselves and overcome emotional challenges.

People who suffer from anxiety and depression are more likely to be self-conscious about their appearance because they may feel that others are criticizing or judging them when they look in the mirror. Despite what others say about them, they may also not see themselves as beautiful or attractive. Often, people who suffer from anxiety do not believe they are worth the effort, so they don't see the point in making an effort to look nice or take care of themselves. People with low self-esteem tend to see themselves as inferior and incompetent compared to others.

This thinking is especially dangerous because it can lead to further problems such as social withdrawal. It can be hard for some people to come out of their shells if they feel that everyone else is more knowledgeable or better-looking than them. People with low self-esteem may feel that they are too different from everyone else, leading some to want to be isolated from society rather than endure this kind of pain for much longer.

Many factors may lead to low self-esteem, and you may suffer from this problem at some point in your life. Low self-esteem can also lead to other serious problems, such as depression, eating disorders, drug or alcohol abuse, and suicide. If you suffer from depression or have been diagnosed with an eating disorder or a mental illness of any kind, please get help. You deserve better than your current situation. Self-esteem is different for everyone, and some people may not have a sense of worthiness in their life. Even if you are not suffering from anxiety or depression now, your self-esteem may plummet in the future if you continue to live the life that you are currently living. It is not a death sentence, and there are things that you can do to help yourself on this journey.

There are many ways to improve self-esteem, but the most important thing is changing your thought patterns. Your thinking patterns affect how you see yourself and how other people see you. When someone has negative thoughts about themselves, it often makes others uncomfortable because those thoughts are usually projected onto others around them. People with low self-esteem tend to compare themselves with others and fail to see their strengths and weaknesses.

"Social phobia" is an emotional experience that involves social situations in which the person develops a high level of anxiety or discomfort when they become afraid that they will act in a way that will embarrass them (or someone else with them) if they are "seen" by other people. This usually starts early in life, between 5-12 years old, but not always. Sometimes, it can come later in life after stressful events or a traumatic injury. When the anxiety becomes intense, it inhibits the child's ability to function well in certain social situations. It commonly occurs in children who are shy or have trouble making friends. Whether it is a single incident or something that builds up over time, the phobic experience will make him feel nervous and anxious if he faces a social situation where he might be judged by someone else.

There are plenty of ways to help your children overcome their fears and develop better coping skills for social anxiety disorder. There are treatments for this disorder, but for those who wait too long before seeking help, the effects can be much harder on the child and his family. One of the most common reasons for a person's fear of social situations is when their self-esteem is low. The person may believe they are not good enough and that others view them similarly. This can lead to feelings of despair, helplessness, and hopelessness, which causes them to withdraw from those around them. This, in turn, leads to feelings of loneliness and depression which further worsens the situation. The person then becomes trapped in a vicious cycle. The individual's level of self-esteem can be improved when they can break out of the cycle. Their thoughts and feelings affect their self-esteem, which a social anxiety disorder may cause.

A common cause of low self-esteem in adolescents is when the child is exposed to painful and traumatic situations at a young age. One of the most common forms of childhood trauma or abuse that can cause low self-esteem in adolescents is sexual abuse. Other types include physical and emotional neglect. An abused child may grow up confused and scared about their identity and even feel abandoned by their parents. When they reach adulthood, this negative emotional state that they experienced in childhood can cause them to lose confidence when they are around other people. This fear may manifest itself in social anxiety disorder. As a result of their traumatic experiences, they may have trouble forming healthy relationships with other people, and they may be afraid of being abandoned again. They may even fear going to work as a result. The question that arises from this is how adolescents can cope with the pain and trauma of childhood abuse. To improve self-esteem in adolescents, it is important to understand that the event does not define them as individuals. Just because the individual went through something traumatic at some point does not mean that they are a bad person. They should be aware of this and attempt to avoid thinking negatively about themselves and others. They should also be aware of the negative thoughts that they are having, such as "people like me." The abuse may cause these that they experienced in childhood. They should then attempt to challenge these thoughts by thinking about something positive and trying to avoid making these memories worse.

Many people experience social anxiety during their teenage years, and some become very fearful of getting close to others, leading to isolation from their peers. A socially anxious individual may feel uncomfortable and shy in social settings, especially when there is a possibility of being judged or ridiculed by others for their actions or appearance. Those who are socially anxious can also experience a great deal of stress and anxiety because of the embarrassment or difficulty they experience during social events. People with a social anxiety disorder may find it hard to make new friends and even miss opportunities they could have used to create other friendships and relationships.

Individuals with social anxiety disorder tend to feel that their performance is unsatisfactory and can suffer from low self-esteem. They may resent that everyone else seems to do things without problems and cannot keep up with them. This is a major cause of low self-esteem in adolescents and social anxiety disorder in adults. This results in individuals losing confidence in their abilities and may even lose enthusiasm for their actions. As a result of this feeling of inferiority, the person may feel that their work is not up to standard and that they are not worthy of praise. Because low self-esteem can lead to other negative effects, such as social anxiety disorder, individuals need to try and improve their self-esteem as soon as possible by fighting against this feeling and replacing it with positive thoughts.

Another reason a person might be afraid when in social situations is that they are being abused by someone else or have been abuse victims in the past. Abuse can take many forms, including physical, sexual, emotional, and psychological abuse. Someone who has been abused will have lower self-esteem, and they may distance themselves from others. They may be more likely to react hostile when around people and feel the abuser is controlling them.

The last reason for social anxiety disorder is how the person's environment has been set up. This includes how their parents avoided situations that were too embarrassing for their child or what kind of punishment a child received if they were caught doing something wrong. These types of punishments can cause a negative association with social situations, which eventually leads to an avoidance of them.

A person with a social anxiety disorder may be unwilling to spend time with others because of the fear of rejection. For example, they fear that if they make friends with someone, their friends will not like them and will not want to be around them. Although it is true that some people are self-centered and aren't interested in others, it is often the case that most people are anxious to make friends quickly but need reassurance from those around them to know how to act.

In some cases, the fears associated with social anxiety disorder lead to a generalized fear of other people.

The stigma of having social anxiety is not just felt by the person suffering from it but also by their friends and family. Many people with this disorder feel that it is a weakness that should be dealt with on one's own. There is a lack of understanding about the true nature of this condition and the seriousness involved in having it. Some of the myths surrounding social anxiety are listed below:

Many people believe that if you feel embarrassed by making a fool of yourself, you must have a panic attack. For example, if someone is about to give a presentation and panics or feels like they are going to vomit or cry (as these are common symptoms), many people still believe that the person has gone mad and have trouble accepting that people can feel this way. It's also found that people with this disorder who have been socially anxious for most of their life usually have other disorders, such as depression.

Many people believe that social anxiety is caused by being too shy or introverted. One of the most effective methods for improving self-esteem is to perform what is known as cognitive restructuring, which involves challenging the negative thoughts that the person is experiencing. They begin by asking themselves why they think or feel a particular way and then attempt to change those thoughts or feelings accordingly. This can help them start acting positively, which will, in turn, improve their confidence level. They can begin to feel better about themselves by changing their attitude and behavior. This can make them less sensitive to the criticism of others and help improve their self-esteem.

Improvement of self-esteem in adolescents by a social anxiety disorder. Other methods for improving self-esteem in adolescents include encouraging them to understand that their opinion is important and that they are not alone. This can be achieved by explaining to them what is happening in their brains at the time. For example, if adolescents fear public speaking, they may feel anxious and confused about why they are experiencing a panic attack when asked to talk to others. They should be encouraged to explain this situation in detail using simple language to avoid confusion.

Another method involves conversing with them and explaining why it is important for them to feel good about themselves. A positive person will always find something positive about themselves, meaning that other people will always find something positive about them too. They should be encouraged to share their strengths with those they know so that they can begin building up their self-esteem.

The last method involves helping them understand that the behavior they have been exhibiting is causing the problems in their social life and not them as individuals. By explaining this to them, they can understand that the people around them are more concerned about what these individuals are doing than who they are. This is a positive motivation for change because it shows them how much others care about them. They should be encouraged to take positive actions in response and overcome any feelings of negative self-worth which may be holding them back from doing so.

Anxiety and depression in adolescents, how to recognize the signs-self harm

The adolescent years may be the most formative period in a person's life, yet they are also the most difficult. This is especially true for teenagers, who must juggle all their responsibilities (friends, academics, family relationships) with their personal development and identity challenges. Problems can arise when one or more of these areas come into conflict; for example, when the needs of parents and adolescents are in conflict. Anxiety and depression in adolescents amount to one of the most common mental disorders among teenagers. This can be due to a few different reasons; these reasons differ depending on the age of the person suffering from anxiety and depression. The different ages are:

Anxiety could be a self-imposed emotion, and it could also be an interpersonal emotion. When it comes to interpersonal anxiety is one that affects persons of the same age or older than themselves. If a teenager faces chronic anxiety disorder, their symptoms could vary in intensity and appearance compared to others suffering from the same condition. Many parents are concerned about children suffering from anxiety and depression, especially those who feel they do not blend in with their peers. Most parents worry about what others think of their son or daughter when they are seen around town or hanging out at parties with other teenagers their age. This is not necessarily negative, but it can seem that way because people tend to associate certain traits with teenage boys and girls that may cause them to dislike them more than they like them.

Depression is an illness identified as a common problem during adolescence. It is estimated that as many as twenty percent of teenagers suffer from depression. The causes for the onset of depression are numerous and include genetic and biological factors and environmental issues. One of the main traits parents may not like about a child suffering from anxiety and depression is their lack of self-confidence. Many individuals will look at a teenager as deathly afraid of other people and size them up as being a coward and lacking self-confidence. They will feel this way because it is easy to assume this if a child suffers from anxiety and depression. The reality is a person who suffers from low self-esteem does not care what others think about them; they have already made up their minds about themselves and do not need others to give them any additional opinions on their appearance or character.

Sometimes teens with anxiety disorders suffer from depression as well. A person with depression does not care about what people think about them, does not smile as much, and is more likely to be seen by others as being quiet or unfriendly. This is why parents should not let their children suffer in silence. If they have any issues with their mental state, they need to talk to someone rather than stay silent. Parents should be the first line of defense in a child's life, and they need to learn how to express themselves properly if they have any issues that need medical attention.

Stress is a factor in the lives of most adolescents. Stress becomes a problem when it is chronic or severe enough to disrupt an individual's ability to function. During adolescence, an individual begins to develop a sense of self separate from family members. During this time, they may begin to evaluate their life in terms of how well they meet their expectations. For many teenagers, this can be a stressful experience in itself.

The onset of puberty can also lead to depression in some cases, as hormone changes cause shifts in mood indicators such as irritability and anxiety. The pressure to conform to stereotypical gender roles can also cause some teenagers, who are unable or unwilling to fit into the roles that they are expected to, to be unhappy. Eighteen is often considered the age when adolescents enter adulthood. Today, many young people are given increased freedoms and responsibilities that may be far beyond their years. This independence can be both exciting and frightening for a teenager, and it is not uncommon for them to experience an identity crisis at this time as they try to forge a personal identity separate from their family life.

Adolescents who suffer from depression may display various

symptoms in addition to those commonly associated with depression in adults. Symptoms include low self-esteem; negative emotional responses; minor depressive symptoms, including restlessness, fatigue, and loss of motivation; lack of concentration and thought processes; and physical manifestations such as unexplained weight gain or a change in appetite.

Depression among adolescents can also be associated with a tendency to engage in behaviors that are harmful to the individual, such as self-harm. This can be manifested as either multiple suicide attempts or initiating self-harm (e.g., cutting) alone or with other individuals (usually peers). Those at risk may also exhibit disorganized thinking, characterized by irrational thoughts and feelings. They are more apt to believe conspiracy theories and lose touch with reality when facing problems.

A characteristic of depression among adolescents is that it often combines with different forms of psychological distress, such as anxiety disorders and eating disorders. It is easy to become focused on the outside world, but a teen left to their own devices, for example, in their bedroom, may feel trapped and see a lot of themselves in the characters they are reading about. This can lead to them feeling extreme self-hatred, which can spiral into suicidal thoughts or attempts. It is also common for teens who suffer from depression to display other symptoms of mood disorders, such as mania or severe depression and anxiety.

Symptoms of depression in teenagers y not always be readily identifiable. In many cases, the symptoms that may indicate depression include nightmares, fear of the dark or staying away from the light, difficulty concentrating, and frequent restlessness.

Depression in children is most common between the ages of 10 and 12. However, age is not a defining factor concerning depression in teens, as studies have shown that even infants under two years old can also suffer from it. Depression in children occurs for many reasons, but experts believe genetics may play a role since mothers who suffer from depression before birth are more likely to have a depressed child. Other factors that have been linked with depression in teens include stressful life events such as parental separation or abuse; physical health problems (e.g.

Depression in children usually develops from changes in the family environment or social pressures. The poor choices made by adolescents with depression can sometimes create long-term problems for their parents. Depression can also lead to low self-esteem, communication, and behavioral problems in children.

Bipolar disorder is when people have alternating periods of excessive moodiness (mania) and depression. It is characterized by a person having periods of joy and being full of energy (mania), combined with low mood and listlessness (depression).

Symptoms of mania include being giddy and having a reduced need for sleep. An individual suffering from mania may also show out-of-character behavior, such as becoming promiscuous or impulsive. Mania is usually accompanied by irritability, racing thoughts, and rapid speech. In contrast to the other symptoms, an individual will experience a mood of low self-esteem when they are depressed. A person suffering from depression may stop participating in activities they previously enjoyed and were first thought to be a sign of laziness may be part of the symptomology.

It has been found that people with higher levels of depression have lower levels of serotonin in the brain, which causes chemical imbalances that make them susceptible to poor moods more often. It is thought that depression can be treated by taking a course of antidepressants. However, some claim that an antidepressant may cause more severe disorders, such as bipolar disorder. Therefore, medication is recommended only in cases where the person suffers from all the symptoms of depression, not just some of them. Still, the aim should be to reduce symptoms rather than to cure them completely.

Depression in children and teenagers can sometimes present as a simple problem, like poor grades or misbehaving in class. However, it may indicate the presence of a much more serious condition.

As with adults, teenagers often find themselves in a crisis over their identity. This can lead to some questioning their existence and whether they have any value as an individual or are truly happy within themselves. Depression can result from these thoughts, manifested as thoughts of suicide or other self-harming behaviors. Adolescents who commit suicide attempts or attempt self-harm understand that these actions will relieve them from the pain they feel inside.

Depression often begins when the teen is very young and may not be apparent to parents or teachers until the child's tenth birthday or later in life. This is because depression may masquerade as various physical or psychological conditions. A child or teen that seems to be experiencing all or any of the following symptoms may be suffering from depression:

Being treated for a condition at a young age can make it easy to forget that there is also the possibility of underlying mental illnesses such as depression, low self-esteem, and other mood issues. Adolescents diagnosed with a physical illness are prone to developing psychological disorders in addition to these conditions. This means that there must be ongoing monitoring and assessment of the adolescent's mental health, especially if they have been diagnosed with a chronically ill condition.

It is not uncommon for depression to have atypical symptoms that can be misconstrued as part of the underlying condition. Also, it is important to note that there are cases when a person's mood can be affected by their underlying condition or disease processes, so both must be monitored if present simultaneously. Because adolescents tend to underreport their feelings and thoughts on emotional issues, parents, teachers, and health professionals need to observe behavioral changes to determine whether or not a child or teen should be assessed by a professional. A child or teen displaying poor performance at school, excessive mood swings, and non-suicidal self-harm should be assessed.

Individuals that suffer from depression are not the same as those that suffer from anxiety. Individuals with depression have tremendous emotional baggage and usually believe something is wrong with them. They will look for answers to their problems internally because they do not trust others and can be very self-conscious about themselves. A person suffering from depression might search for medical help or consult a counselor or therapist to find out what other people think about them and their situation. If the teen is displaying any of the following, then it is recommended that they speak with a professional. However, if a teenager displays many of these symptoms for an extended period, then it is recommended that professional guidance and therapy be sought earlier:

Several factors in life may create a suitable environment for developing adolescent depression. These include the family dynamic, peer influence, educational environments, and stress.

Adolescents that have been diagnosed with bipolar disorder have been found to have higher instances of depression than those without the diagnosis of bipolar disorder. Studies have also indicated that mood disorders in children and teenagers can severely impact their health and development.

Studies have shown that parents with bipolar disorder have a higher incidence of depression than parents without a diagnosis of bipolar disorder. However, the association between children and adolescents with mood disorders, specifically bipolar disorder, is inconsistent across studies. Most studies indicate no apparent link between children and adolescents with mood disorders, but some suggest an increased likelihood of suicidal behavior. This is a big question that needs to be answered as it has severe implications for people affected by these conditions and their families and caregivers.

When depression goes untreated, it can have long-term effects on both physical and mental health.

The following exercise was designed to allow you to take control of your life by becoming more aware of your actions and motivations.

"Take the time to consider each question before answering, and be as honest and open with yourself as possible."

1. How would you describe yourself?

_____

_____

_____

_____

_____

_____

_____

_____

2. What do you like about yourself?

_____

_____

_____

_____

_____

_____

_____

_____

3. What are your strengths?

_____

_____

_____

_____

_____

_____

_____

_____

4. What are your weaknesses?

_____

_____

_____

_____

_____

_____

_____

_____

5. Where have you found happiness in the past? (Known or unknown)_____

_____

_____

_____

_____

_____

6. Where is happiness for you now
(Known or
unknown)_____

_____

_____

_____

_____

_____

7. Describe how you feel about
yourself.

_____

_____

_____

_____

_____

_____

_____

_____

8. How do your friends feel about you? (Known or unknown)_____

_____

_____

_____

_____

_____

9. What are some of your hobbies? (Known or unknown)_____

_____

_____

_____

_____

_____

10. What do you like to do in your spare time? (Known or unknown)_____

_____

_____

Eating disorder

Eating disorders, also known as eating dysfunctions, are a group of conditions characterized by abnormal eating habits that can have several detrimental effects on health. Disturbances in eating habits may result from social, cultural, and biological factors. The most common eating disorders are anorexia nervosa and bulimia nervosa; however, binge-eating disorder is a recently identified condition that has emerged in recent years. Other eating disorders include pica, rumination disorder, avoidant/restrictive food intake disorder (ARFID), and orthorexia Nervosa.

Several factors play a role in the development of an eating disorder.

They include biological, psychological, social, and cultural influences. People develop eating disorders for different reasons. However, one of the most common contributing factors is an individual's desire to obtain complete control over as many aspects of their life as possible. This is a desire that most people possess to some degree; however, people with eating disorders have this need met in an unhealthy manner at the expense of their health and well-being.

Eating disorders are not caused by something a mother did or didn't do during pregnancy. These eating disorders are life-threatening and can cause serious harm. They are often related to low self-esteem, conflicts, issues with body image, fear of becoming overweight, and other issues that many teens face today. Many teens suffer from depression, another reason for increased eating disorders. Some teens also have trouble with panic attacks, anxiety disorders, and social phobia because of their low self-esteem and body image issues. They feel they can't live up to everyone else's ideal version of themselves and resort to trying to be perfect in other ways. This may also lead to substance abuse problems because they can't handle being judged by others.

What can you do to lower your child's risk of developing eating disorders?

The most important thing is to talk to your children about body image and get them to help if they think they may have an eating disorder. Many lifelong problems accompany eating disorders, including serious emotional issues and starvation. It is important to have support groups or counselors to talk with your child or teen. You may even want to talk to your pediatrician about how you can help prevent this from happening in your family.

Eating disorders usually occur during adolescence when individuals are more conscious of how they look, feel about themselves, and fit in socially. The prevalence of eating disorders is higher in females than in males. Approximately 1% to 3% of females aged 12–19 years have developed an eating disorder at some point in their life, and approximately 0.5% to 1% of males in the same age group exhibit this issue. It has also been found that up to one-third of adolescents with an eating disorder have also engaged in self-harm or attempted suicide.

Eating disorders are associated with several psychological and physical complications and increased symptoms of depression, anxiety, or substance abuse among both females and males, which could lead to serious issues such as death (through dangerous behaviors performed by individuals with eating disorders). Some disorders may not be as serious, however, such as bulimia nervosa. This condition is associated with a number of dangerous behaviors, such as purging or fasting. It has been found to have long-term consequences for many people who suffer from it.

Several risk factors involved in developing eating disorders in adolescents can affect their health and well-being. These include personality traits such as perfectionism and low self-esteem and peer relationships with individuals who show signs of vulnerability to an eating disorder; however, other factors that play a role in the development of eating disorders are biological.

The biological factors that can play a role in the development of eating disorders include genetics and brain chemistry. Certain genes are linked to eating disorders, such as the BINGO gene, a genetic sequence on chromosome 7 responsible for about 70 percent of anorexia nervosa. Other genes associated with eating disorders include serotonin production (5-HT) and serotonin receptors, found on chromosome 2q33. Serotonin has been linked to the development of eating disorders, as lowering serotonin levels and increasing elevated levels may impact the condition.

Brain chemistry can also contribute to the development of eating disorders. It is believed that abnormalities in brain chemistry may contribute to eating disorders, especially as they relate to serotonin and serotonin receptors. While it is still being studied, it is thought that certain abnormalities in brain chemistry may contribute to the development of eating disorders such as irritability, frustration, and anger. These emotions could potentially play a role in developing an eating disorder.

Some biological factors play a role in developing teenage and adolescent eating disorders. However, some risk factors may predispose people to develop these conditions. These include genetics and brain chemistry. Individuals who show signs of vulnerability to an eating disorder may also show signs of other conditions, such as depression or anxiety.

The prevalence of eating disorders in adolescents is about 5.8%. Among females, the prevalence is 9%; however, it is 1% among males. The risk factors associated with eating disorders are not limited to biological factors, which can play a role in developing these conditions. Some personality traits can predispose people to develop eating disorders, but the individuals who fit this category often do so without their conscious awareness

Social anxiety disorder is closely related to an eating disorder, and some people may find that they struggle with both at the same time. Socially anxious people often avoid situations where they are the center of attention. They may drop out of clubs or draw crowds of people to them when they go out in public, creating a feeling of extreme social isolation. If you have a child, this could create a lot more stress for you emotionally because you feel like your child isn't able to form friendships or has problems with self-image. If you have ever suffered from anxiety and understand your feelings, you can help teach your children coping abilities through activities such as exposure therapy.

Some people have the genetics to be more socially anxious than others, but being more socially anxious does not mean that suddenly you will develop an eating disorder. You should look into both of these disorders if you have any kind of the symptoms or if you're beginning to develop emotional issues.

The following exercise will guide you through the diagnostic assessment to determine if you have an eating disorder. Answer "yes" or "no" to each question and tally your responses, which will help determine whether or not you are suffering from an eating disorder for which you might want to seek treatment.

Adult supervision is required for this exercise.

1. Are you worried about your weight?

2. Do you fear gaining or becoming fat despite being underweight?

3. Do you dislike how you look in photographs?

4. Have thoughts about food or eating that make you feel bad?

5. Are you always afraid of gaining weight?

6. Do you need to skip meals or eat very little food?

How to improve relationships with classmates and sport

This chapter is aimed at helping you understand your teenager, why they may be acting out of character, and how to help them. You must ascertain what type of behavior they are exhibiting and why, so you can recognize their problem emotions and take action to help them deal with them. When it comes to school and sports, many people feel like they aren't good enough. It may be because of certain things that have happened in the past or because you feel nervous about a situation.

The first step in solving problems is clearly understanding the situation or what is happening behind the scenes. By reading this chapter of the book, you should be able to understand how your teenager's problem emotions are affecting them. School and sports can become much more difficult when a student struggles with social anxiety disorder. While academic performance may suffer and how they relate to their teachers and classmates can also be affected, there are ways to help improve things. The following are some tips that can help make school and sports easier for anyone who struggles with social anxiety disorder.

Tips to help with school work:

Students struggling with a social anxiety disorder may either not ask anyone for help or may become overwhelmed by asking for help. For this reason, it is important to have resources available for your child to ask for guidance without worrying about being singled out or the answer being incorrect. Asking for help and studying in a group can give students more self-confidence.

If your child is struggling in school and sports due to social anxiety disorder, they must find an activity they are good at but enjoy. This will help feed their confidence and self-esteem and give them a sense of purpose. A fun activity that helps you grow and become better at something can help build your self-esteem and social confidence.

Many students are put in a situation where they feel like they are the center of attention when they have to do an oral report or present in front of the class. For socially anxious students, these situations can be very stressful. If you have a child who struggles with this, try to talk to their teacher about group projects, group presentations, etc.

Social anxiety disorder can make it hard for someone to relate to others as easily. Try to create a comfortable and peaceful environment for your child to be able to concentrate. To do this, you may consider having a professional massage therapist involves your child. This will help relax them and make them more receptive to socializing.

Jaclyn has struggled with how she relates to those around her because she thinks they don't understand or believe her when she tells them about her anxiety and social anxiety disorder. When Jaclyn realized someone close was also struggling with this, their friendship became a lot easier. Now they try not to keep up the idea of what they can't do; rather, they try to focus on everything they can do in their situation. To help another family struggling with this, discuss that you can always give support when needed, if not from a professional or someone close, then from someone they know who has struggled with this. It is important to realize that no matter what you do, your child will never be able to change their social anxiety disorder. You should accept it and move forward in a positive direction.

Tips to help with sports:

Your child must understand that the whole point of school and sports is to build relationships with others.

School and sports can create many different stressors for students who struggle with social anxiety disorder due to their anxieties. If they get awkward in a sports situation, they may begin to worry that they will be accused of not giving it their all. This can lead to great self-doubt and sometimes depression. It is a good idea for the student to talk about their feelings with the coach if they have any doubts. The coach's main goal is to help the student understand any social anxiety disorder, but also help him, or her improve their performance through playing their sport more often and making an effort on the field.

The more confident students are in themselves, the more confident they will be able to control situations where others are looking at them. Students will realize they can do it and shouldn't be so concerned about misjudging people. Players who have trouble with their development or performance in sports are often not competitive. Rather, they are competitive because they just want to do better. They are often more afraid of being judged by the coach if they don't do as well as others. This player must find an activity where they can feel like a winner and not a loser, such as brain teasers or strength training exercises.

Relating with others is an essential part of life, whether you realize it or not. Without relationships, it would be like walking alone with no one to relate to. You may have been raised in a situation where you didn't have a lot of friends, or you may just feel like you aren't as social as others. These are issues that can be helped by joining a club at school related to something that interests you and creating friendships based on something other than your social anxiety disorder. When you have a child who struggles with social anxiety disorder, and they are on the school sports team, this can be very stressful. Sports can be a great way to bond with friends, but it can also create a lot of stress. This is because it puts your child in an uncomfortable social situation which can cause them to feel isolated. While Jaclyn was on her basketball team, she knew that she was better than the rest at some things, like shooting baskets or defense. To help build up her self-confidence, even more, she would practice by herself and do what she does best without the pressure of being in front of others. Some people have to be put in front of the group, but others will also never have to be put in front of a group. Remember this because your child must find something they love and do well at, no matter how big or small it may seem.

Social anxiety disorder can make it hard for anyone to relate to others, but when you treat your social anxiety disorder as normal, there is nothing to be afraid of. A person with social anxiety disorder relates to others like someone without a social anxiety disorder does. The only difference is that someone with an addiction has an addiction, and someone with a social anxiety disorder has a social anxiety disorder.

When a student deals with these issues in school or at the gym, it may be hard for them to relate. This may cause them not to want to go out anymore or lose touch with the people they are close with. If you are struggling with social anxiety disorder, school, or sports, and nobody understands what you're going through, try joining another club or sport you might enjoy. This will help your self-esteem grow and give you a sense of accomplishment when growing as an athlete. It can be hard for people with a social anxiety disorder who are also athletes or students in school to relate to their teammates or teachers because they feel like they are always judged. When this happens, it can be difficult for the student not only academically but socially as well.

If you are a student with social anxiety disorder in school, you may be able to work on it by participating in extracurricular activities. These can include art, music classes, or even sports at your school. If you don't have extracurricular activities, online activities are available. This will help you learn to be more comfortable around people and regularly attend school. Also, making friends and being comfortable with your school culture is important.

If you are going through a difficult time in your life and you feel like you have social anxiety disorder all the time, this may be due to other issues such as depression or eating disorders. Also, a person with a social anxiety disorder struggling with drug or alcohol abuse has a harder time adjusting socially. Some things may be causing stress, such as relationships at school or work, family issues, and legal problems. A person dealing with these stresses will find it more difficult to work on their symptoms of social anxiety disorder. These individuals may try to hide their symptoms from others because they don't want others to think they have problems. They may keep the anxiety to themselves or try to confide in somebody else, who will probably dismiss their thoughts.

If your child is dealing with social anxiety disorder in any area of life, try to encourage them to take some time off from what they're doing and do something that they enjoy instead. Teens who suffer from symptoms of this condition often experience many issues with school performance, relationships with classmates, and even sports performance. In sports, many people find that if they are not at the top of their game, it can make them feel very frustrated or depressed, leading to even more anxiety. Sometimes, having a coach who understands the situation can make all the difference for an athlete with an eating disorder or other mental illness.

School performance is another important part of being healthy. While our academics are important, it can be harder to show what we do in school to our parents and the world around us. We may feel inferior or less than others in school because those other students seem much better than us. Because we're busy in-class learning and not paying attention to how other people perceive us, we may miss out on some opportunities that could help us become more positive people.

If we don't feel good enough, we might want to do something about it. We may try to improve our academic performance by studying more, cheating on tests, or not handing in homework assignments. Studies found that people who cheat on tests usually come from lower-income families. Students who are wealthier and in the higher income bracket have a greater propensity for cheating. It seems that students from wealthier backgrounds have the resources available to buy their way through college without worrying about paying attention in class or even cheating on tests as much as someone who is struggling financially.

Many sports coaches have found out the hard way that many students begin to struggle in their first year of high school. If they don't get good grades, they might try to improve their situation by cheating on tests or not handing in assignments. This is why many sports coaches hire tutors and math coaches for their athletes and pay close attention to their grades. Even if you don't have a sport in school, there are still skills that you can practice to help your academics. For some reason, people without academic success tend to take classes they do not enjoy. They fill time with classes they hate to increase their GPA. This can help you learn how to determine what classes you like and what you don't.

There are several ways to ensure that your academic performance is the best. The first way is by knowing what your goals are in school and being constantly aware of them. You may change over time if you don't have specific goals when you start. A big part of success at school and sports is feeling confident and happy about yourself. The more confident you are, the easier it will be for you to succeed in your course or match.

If you feel nervous about something, it will only make you feel worse about yourself when the time comes for you to try again, so do your best to overcome these thoughts before they get out of hand. You should also feel confident about yourself and what you have accomplished in your life; otherwise, you will always feel down about something. When you feel negative or nervous about something, think of all the great things you have done or achieved in your life, even if it is not compared to others.

Remember that everyone goes through struggles, and sometimes there is nothing wrong with being unsure. You may struggle with a few things but remember that you will get over them as long as you keep going and push yourself repeatedly until they are over. There are times when some people may find it hard to maintain this positive mindset and come across as negative. If you feel this is the case with you, then make sure you change the way you think by looking at all the positive points in your life. You should take a moment to acknowledge these things because often, we get caught up with what we do not have and forget to appreciate what we do have.

You should also give yourself some time every day to either sit and reflect on your actions, talk about them with someone or write it down in a diary. Sometimes just writing down all of your thoughts will help you to clear your mind, understand yourself better and move forwards

Generalized anxiety disorder-memory difficulties-sleep disorder

Anxiety disorders are a group of mental illnesses that can make you feel afraid, worried, or uneasy. When severe, these feelings can be disabling and interfere with your work, school, and social life. Generalized anxiety disorder is persistent and excessive worry about recurring life events. In contrast to normal "worries" about day-to-day activities that may come up from time to time, the worries experienced by people with GAD are more intense and uncontrollable. Individuals who suffer from generalized anxiety disorder (GAD) often experience the following symptoms:

1. Feeling on edge or easily fatigued

2. Restlessness and being easily irritated, impatient

3. Difficulty concentrating; difficulty completing tasks

4. Irritability or muscle tension

5. Lack of energy and fatigue

Socially anxious individuals have an exaggerated fear of embarrassment and humiliation in social situations, which often results in people with social anxiety avoiding social events where they fear being judged by others because they fear that they will act in a socially embarrassing way. In the same way that there is a genetic predisposition for generalized anxiety disorder, there is also a genetic link to memory problems. One study has found that those experiencing social anxiety are more likely to suffer from short-term or long-term memory problems.

Social anxiety disorder has been prevalent in clinical and community populations. It has a significant incidence in the two most common psychiatric disorders, i.e., mood and anxiety disorders. In addition, social anxiety is associated with many other problems, such as substance abuse and depression, and can be related to physical illnesses, such as cardiovascular disease or gastrointestinal problems. Social anxiety disorder is not just a problem of independent living but also close relationships. It is also related to suicide and suicidal ideation (the tendency to think about suicide). Social phobia has been linked with low self-esteem, negative self-evaluation, poor interpersonal relationships, limited social support networks, increased depressive symptoms, and dissociative experiences that are often associated with childhood abuse experiences

Studies have shown that social anxiety disorder often experiences negative emotions and thoughts. These thoughts include feelings of depression, anxiety, fear, and physical discomfort while they are in social situations. Those suffering from memory loss and no prior history of depression or anxiety are more likely to be diagnosed with a generalized anxiety disorder than those who did not cope well with stress.

According to a study published in Anxiety Research and Therapy, you are more likely to have a lower IQ if you suffer from a social anxiety disorder. The study also found that people diagnosed with a social anxiety disorder had trouble with memory recall and making decisions.

This finding supports that those experiencing social anxiety have an upscale of temporary memory problems when they develop depression and other disorders. All parents need to be aware of their child's symptoms to identify whether or not the disorder is happening early on. The very nature of anxiety disorders is that they are difficult to identify and make it to the proper diagnosis. Social anxiety disorder symptoms can include a wide range of symptoms, such as:

- Anxious thoughts, fears, nervousness, and physical discomfort.

- Feeling as if one is being watched or judged by others.

- Feeling as if their speech is not good enough or that people are thinking about them.

- Fear of public speaking or other public situations.

These symptoms can be similar to those experienced by those who struggle with depression. Still, the difference between anxiety disorders and depression is how you feel after being in certain situations for a long time. You can be generally anxious but feel better about the situation if you can cope and not let it affect your emotions. On the other hand, if you are suffering from a social anxiety disorder, your anxiety may only get worse as time goes on.

As mentioned before, there is a genetic link between generalized anxiety disorder and depression. Those with both of these disorders are more likely to experience depression after experiencing generalized anxiety for a long time. According to a study done by the National Institute of Mental Health (NIMH), people who suffer from generalized anxiety disorder report higher levels of suicidal thoughts than those that do not have this disorder.

Anyone who suffers from generalized anxiety disorder has a higher risk of developing other mental health problems. What are these other mental health problems? The emotional and social effects that those suffering from generalized anxiety disorder experience can also extend to their family members and friends.

What happens when your child is struggling in school because of anxiety?

What happens when your child struggles in school because of another mental health disorder?

Depression and anxiety can devastate a child's self-esteem and affect their confidence and ability to perform well in school. If you have children, supporting them through their academic or extracurricular activities is important. The goal should be to maintain at least an average grade point average while they are experiencing an increase in anxiety or depression. This will help to prevent them from falling behind in school.

Children with generalized anxiety disorder need to receive treatment and support from the family members around them.

The term "social anxiety disorder" implies that a person with the disorder has an abnormally strong fear of social situations and interactions, which causes severe emotional distress. Symptoms of this disorder include blushing, sweating, trembling, difficulty speaking, rapid heartbeat or irregular heart rate, nausea, dry mouth (known as GAD - Generalized Anxiety Disorder), or feeling faint. Several internal and external responses to social anxiety can help decrease the severity of the feelings of fear and embarrassment during your next social situation. The following techniques focus on changing your perception and not the situation itself.

To reduce your anxiety during a social situation, you must realize that your performance is not being judged as harshly as you think. When you realize your performance in a social situation is not being judged by others as you had thought, you will be less likely to feel paranoid and anxious. Changing your perception of what other people think about you makes it easier to relax in a social setting. Those who suffer from a social anxiety disorder are more likely to experience flashbacks while experiencing a fearful situation or in the form of nightmares. If this is the case, it should be addressed immediately with a therapist or psychiatrist so they can work through their fears and learn how to manage them.

When a person has a worry disorder such as social anxiety, the repetitive thoughts can get so overwhelming that it's difficult for anyone to function normally. Anxious behaviors are also common because these thoughts are typically accompanied by physical symptoms such as sweating and increased heart rate. This makes people feel trapped by the experience and doesn't allow them to feel comfortable in social situations where they may not be asked many questions or judged harshly – the key triggers of anxiety. By breaking the repetitive cycle of negative thoughts – which often lead to avoidance of situations that may trigger worry and anxiety – therapy can help people with their social anxiety.

When people feel like their physical health is at risk, their social life and relationships are likely to suffer. People suffering from social anxiety disorder may become socially isolated and have problems in relationships, work, school, and other activities. This type of anxiety is mostly found in adults who have undergone some traumatic event or are currently experiencing stressful situations that they feel they can't control.

Social Anxiety Disorder can be treated with psychotherapy (also called "talk therapy") or medication. Psychotherapy aims to help people learn tools and skills to manage their social anxiety. Psychotherapy is commonly combined with medication because it's effective for many people with this disorder. People with social anxiety may benefit from cognitive behavioral therapy, which focuses on helping people change how they view themselves and what they believe will happen in social situations. The best way to treat generalized anxiety disorder is to identify the symptoms of their anxiety and address them directly by taking simple steps. Realizing that their behavior is out of control and that they can learn to control fear and embarrassment may make people more confident in social situations. Living life without fear and embarrassment can be possible for people suffering from the disorder.

In conclusion, the most common mental health problem experienced by teenagers is anxiety. It affects 6.5

million children in America alone. The symptoms vary among children but typically start with worry about being different from other kids. This anxiety can lead to many physical effects like panic attacks, stomach-churning, sweating, giddiness, or heart palpitations (if it gets worse, it could lead to a full-blown panic attack). If this is not addressed early, it can lead to social problems that could affect a child's life by the time they are 4 or 5 years of age. This disorder often leads to panic attacks. However, if it is treated early enough, children can easily control it. It has been studied and determined that children with anxiety have stronger SSRI gene expression in their brains, thus leading them to develop anxiety disorders more quicker.

Anxiety disorders are common among people diagnosed with an eating disorder. The two most common eating disorders are anorexia and bulimia. The diagnosis of social anxiety disorder occurs in about 10-15% of people with anorexia nervosa. In addition to the symptoms of social anxiety that occur in people with social anxiety disorder, people with anorexia nervosa have other symptoms related to their eating disorder. These other symptoms include excessive concern about becoming fat and a fear of gaining weight even while they are underweight; these symptoms can cause people to be afraid to eat or become more anxious when they eat. These people will also be preoccupied with food and weight, which interferes with their daily activities (work, school). People with anorexia nervosa can be afraid to eat and avoid social situations, resulting in a lack of social contact. The essential features of social anxiety disorder are severe anxiety in social situations, fear and avoidance of these situations, and an inability to function during these situations. Since people with anorexia nervosa have emotional awareness issues and believe they are overweight (and therefore unworthy), this disorder will likely be present. Diagnosis is made through a structured interview, including previous eating history (i.e., vomiting, bulimia) and use of laxatives or purging behaviors. The diagnosis of comorbid disorders is based on a thorough clinical evaluation.

Social anxiety disorder is often comorbid with other anxiety and mood disorders. A study by Kessler, Berglund, Demler, Jin, and Walters found that social anxiety disorder comorbidity is prevalent in clinical samples but also occurs widely in community samples. The most common disorders that occur with social anxiety are depression and alcohol dependence. Although specific diagnoses are not required to classify a comorbid disorder, studies have shown that people with social anxiety disorder often experience several problems at once. In one study (reported by Stinson), 10% of people with social phobia did not exhibit any other criterion-defined psychiatric condition besides social phobia.

Although anxiety disorders are not incurable, treatment is available to help people live with their anxiety. In many cases, medication is helpful, such as a benzodiazepine (e.g., diazepam), to help reduce anxiety. Other medications may work well with therapy. Cognitive behavioral therapy (CBT) is a form of psychotherapy that focuses on the thought processes that have caused the individual's excessive worry and symptoms of social anxiety disorder. CBT uses several techniques to help people change their negative expectations and develop new ways of thinking that do not lead to excessive worry or anxiety in social situations. This therapy can also be combined with other therapies.

Shyness is associated with an increased risk for social anxiety, and it has long been suggested that shy individuals have disturbed reward systems. One study showed greater activation in the ventral striatum in shy participants than in non-shy participants while watching an interaction between two models who received the money. Another study has shown that shy people had lower "drive" than non-shy people and were less likely to engage in behaviors that would increase their reward levels (such as eating). This is especially true for food consumption, which for most people, is a reward.

With the help of these tests/exercises, you can find out if you suffer from social anxiety. Answer the questions indicated by the "YES" or "NO."

Adult supervision is required for this exercise.

1. Have you ever felt on edge or easily fatigued?

2. Do you have difficulty concentrating in school?

3. Are there insensitive things people say about others?

4. Is it hard for you to understand other people's feelings?

5. Are you easily irritated and impatient?

6. Is it hard for you to get along with people?

7. Do you have difficulty understanding things happening in the world?

8. Are you easily stressed out?

9. Do you avoid responsibilities for fear of failure?

10. Are you too self-conscious and worried about what other people think of you?

11. Do you feel easily embarrassed and humiliated in social situations?

Fun exercises to improve relationships

A social relationship is any of the interactions we have with other people. Our relationships with friends, family and even strangers are all examples of social relationships.

We need to work on our social relationships because they are an important part of life. We spend a lot of time interacting with others in different settings, and it's really important that those interactions go well so we can develop friendships, have meaningful conversations, and find love. It's also good for us because we feel better about ourselves when other people like us or approve of what we're doing somehow. Being confident in yourself is important as it makes you feel good and secure when talking to others. It is important to remember that if you feel comfortable with yourself and have a clear goal, others will respect that and accept your decisions.

One of the most important things people need in their lives is good relationships with others they can depend on. For adolescents to have good relationships, they need to talk comfortably about feelings and problems without having negative thoughts cloud their minds. To help improve their relationships, adolescents should be confident, feel secure in themselves, listen carefully to what people are saying, and express themselves clearly but calmly. If your relationship with another person is poor, you may wish to go on a long walk and talk about the problem or write down your feelings about the person. It is also important to be honest, and tell someone when they are not being friendly or helpful.

A few basic ways you can improve your relationships include:

> Enjoy yourself and be happy!
> Smile when talking to others.
> Listen carefully when talking with other people. Remember what they have said so that you can remind them later if you need to, but don't interrupt them while they are speaking.

Breathe deeply and slowly before you speak to help you express yourself clearly.

When you are in a bad mood, try not to think about it because it will not help. Try thinking about other people who may be worse off and how they deal with their problems. If you can't think of anyone, think of a pet or a friendly person similar to the person you don't like. This will help your mind to focus on positive thoughts, which will help you to feel more relaxed and reduce any negative thoughts that may be clouding your mind. If you are unsure what to say, try asking open questions that will allow you to express your thoughts; it may be easier to answer in this way if you have time to think. This can also be helpful if you have a lot of ideas that you want the other person to hear at once.

When in a difficult situation, it can be useful to ask yourself, "What is the worst that could happen?" or "What was I thinking?" If either of these questions helps, go with this thought, but tell yourself that you will come back later and think about what would happen even though it might not be too pleasant.

We're not always happy with our relationships, though. Sometimes they're harsh, and they can leave us feeling tired and unhappy. At other times, our relationships seem fine, but we're afraid that others won't like us or will be irritated by how we do things. Sometimes people are afraid of being rejected by others or don't have a lot of confidence in their ability to get along with other people. Sometimes people don't feel that others will like them or accept them for who they are. Another reason is that the person may somehow think that everyone is judging them. These are just some of the many reasons why people with social anxiety may fear what might happen if they talk to others. Another

Because we have so many different relationships, it's important to be able to improve all of them. That way, we can feel better about ourselves and have more friendships and more meaningful conversations with others. The purpose of this chapter is to look at ways you can improve your relationships with friends and family members and also develop new friendships by taking action by doing something small like writing a letter or signing up for a class that's offered at your college or university.

Taking action means doing something even when you're afraid of what might happen. It means taking the first step even though you feel nervous. The action you take can be small at first, but as it helps your social anxiety, it will get bigger and help you feel better about yourself. To begin taking action, look around at some of the people in your classes. Make a list of 5–10 people you've sat next to or talked with. Then go through the list and see who might be a good person to say hello to next time you're in class.

Next time you're in a place where you're going to be around other people for a few minutes, say hello to the person on your list who you think would be a good person to talk with.

If one of the people on your list is particularly good at talking with others, go up and introduce yourself.

It doesn't matter if they don't have time to talk now because it's no big deal that you just stopped by. You can say, "Hi! I know it's last minute, but I just wanted to stop by and introduce myself." Or, "You seemed nice, so I wanted to stop by and introduce myself. What are you doing later?" Then smile, give a little wave, and move on.

If you see someone on the list who you know doesn't like talking to others, don't approach them. If it's okay with them, you could email or text that person in case they might be willing to talk to you in the future. You can also do what we call an indirect intervention—see if they'll help you out with something so that they're forced to talk to you a little bit.

Say hi to strangers you see in your classes- The same goes for saying hello to strangers you see in the room. You might ask, "Are you new here?" Or, "I know this is last minute, but I was wondering if you...?" Then smile and move on.

If someone gets nervous or tense when they meet with others, they don't know, and you can say something like, "Oh, it's no problem. I'm Peter." Or, "It's not a big deal if you don't want to talk right now. Let me buy you a coffee or something so we can get to know each other. It's no big deal if you can't talk right now."

Say hi to new people in your classes- Similarly, you can say hello to someone you just saw in a class and say hello to new people. It's no big deal if they don't know you or if they don't want to talk at this time. You can say, "Hi! I'm John. I haven't gotten the chance yet to introduce myself. Something about fearing others and being scared of talking in general: I've been dealing with social anxiety for a long time, and it's something that I'm still working on every day. I hope we can talk again soon." it's such a good thing to have this book because it helps with anxiety. I've learned a lot from it, and it's changed how I approach my social interactions. It's even helped me get into my classes on time. I can't tell you how much of a difference this book has made in my life.

If someone gets nervous and can't talk immediately, you could say something like, "Hey! I just wanted to stop by and say hi! If you need help with

anything, let me know. My name is...
What are you studying? Does your
subject have anything to do with...?"
And then smile and move on.

Social relationships are an important
part of our lives. They offer us a sense
of belonging and purpose and fulfill
the need to feel appreciated and
valued. But if we have social anxiety,
this part of our lives may be very
difficult. It can be hard to enjoy time
with others when we worry
excessively about how they will judge
us or fear that we'll do something
embarrassing or humiliating in
public.

The exercises in this chapter will help
you improve your relationships by
practicing different skills that boost
your confidence and make you more
comfortable interacting socially.

Exercise 1

Start the morning by having a ten-second conversation with the person who wakes you up. How can you gain some extra confidence from your ten-second chat?

Exercise 2

When going out for dinner, seek a table where only you and one other person will sit. Make sure to check a few times during the meal if others are joining you. Imagine that you're not worried about what others think of you and instead enjoy chatting with another person about this or that.

Exercise 3

Prepare for your next meal party by getting some ice cubes from the freezer. Bring them with you, but don't let anyone else know they're there. See how fast you can melt them.

Exercise 4

At the dinner table, ask your friend to describe something that makes them feel very shy. Then ask them to sit at a nearby table and describe the situation.

Exercise 5

While at the dinner party, say hi if you see an attractive woman across the room. Tell her you're embarrassed by your social anxiety and wondering if she was having a good time. Tell her it would be great if she came over and joined you two for a chat so that we can get to know each other better and laugh together some more.

Exercise 6

When you're on the phone with your friends, practice being confident and having fun while discussing ordinary things. For example, one of your best friends might say, "I guess I'm playful because I went out and bought ice cream this evening."

Exercise 7

Talk with a friend about what makes you shy in bed. For example, "I can't relax until the other person has said everything they need to say before we start," or "I get so nervous that I have to be on the top right away."

Exercise 8

Stand up and walk around at lunchtime. See how long it takes to calm down and return to your seat.

Exercise 9

Go to a school assembly, for example, the annual graduation ceremony, and try simply being present. Pretend you don't know anyone there and just enjoy the event.

Exercise 10

For two days, take a piece of paper out of your wallet and write down one thing that makes you more confident. Carry this with you every time you go out.

Exercise 11

When meeting new people, ask them to tell you something their friends have said about them personally or in their group of friends. Write it down on paper so you can refer back to it later if necessary.

Exercise 12

Ask a friend to help you pretend that you're not shy. You only talk to strangers when they come and talk with you. Give each other various instances in which this might happen, like "I'm sure she must still be embarrassed on the bus when we see her again," or "I'm sure he must be nervous when he talks with the girl he met at the bar last week."

Exercise 13

Go out for dinner with a friend and have them invite someone new to join you. Have your friend make some casual conversation with this person. Try to pretend that you don't know them at all, but act pleasantly surprised that they're coming along for dinner.

Exercise 14

Take a friend with you to the movie theatre and ask them to pay for your ticket.

Exercise 15

Pretend that you need to get into a specific nightclub. Practice how you might go to the bouncer and talk with them so they'll let you in.

Exercise 16

One of your friends is struggling with shyness when talking during class. You can help by asking this friend what makes them more comfortable. Then, try taking notes in class while they talk about different things that make them nervous.

Exercise 17

Ask your friend if they would be willing to model a few of your social skills when chatting with friends. For example, they might say, "I'm nervous when I get up in front of people to give a speech. But I practice speaking in front of others and relaxing with friends so that this doesn't bother me anymore. And sometimes it can help to play minor roles, like pretending that I'm talking with my favorite movie star or famous musician."

Exercise 18

The next time you're at a party and see an attractive person across the room, look up and smile. Wave and then take a few steps in their direction. When you see them look up, smile, and wave back, keep walking towards them and introduce

yourself with, "Hi, my name is
_____. I see we're both here by
ourselves. Would you like to join me
for a drink?"

Exercise 19

Ask your friend if you can practice
with them what you'd say when
someone asks for money on the street.
Your friend might say, "I'm sorry, but
I don't have any money." Practice this
together until it feels comfortable to
react in this way when people ask us
for spare change. Then, when you're
out together, practice how to react if
someone asks this question again.

Exercise 20

If you're having a meal at a
restaurant, ask your friend to watch
the table in front of you. You simply
sit by them, order what you want, and

watch the actions of others around you without letting your nervous feeling show.

Meditation exercises for adolescents

The awareness of being distracted is the primary step for being in the present moment. Meditation boosts concentration and focus, which helps to develop a person's sense of self and objectives. It also improves a person's emotional intelligence and allows them to make better judgments in difficult situations.

Meditation is a form of relaxation that helps the mind and body focus on breathing and peaceful thoughts instead of all the stresses in their life. Different types of meditation suit adolescents. They include:

- Mindfulness
- Guided Imagery
- Mantras

Meditation reduces stress in the body and clears the mind, allowing adolescents to understand themselves and their problems more clearly. The first step to meditation is sitting comfortably with both feet on the ground. This will help you relax as it puts your body in a comfortable position. Next, breathe slowly and consciously, allowing your mind to focus on your breath moving in and out of the body. It will allow you to forget the outside world and concentrate on the moment. If you practice meditation regularly, it will help your mind and body relax and reduce mental stress. It is a crucial way to improve health and well-being.

Mantras (Rhymes) Meditation

Mantras are words that have positive or empowering messages that can help you focus your thoughts on positive things in your life or what you want to accomplish in the future. Mantras help to relax your mind and calm the body, which can help you focus on your thoughts and keep them calm. Mantras are words that you repeat to yourself which have a calming effect. They do not have to be said in a foreign language or incantation, but rather just repeating something while calming your mind.

This is an example of a mantra: Breathe in red and breathe out the color blue.

This will encourage you to focus on positive thoughts. It will be easier to relax and feel safe if you believe what you say is true or if you honestly believe in it. This helps distract you from negative thinking processes once again.

Meditation exercises help adolescents stay calm, relaxed, and focused on what they want to achieve. These exercises are used with psychotherapy and can be helpful if used correctly. Guided Imagery is a type of guided meditation that uses imagery to help you relax, focus on your breathing, and calm your mind. The first step is to find a comfortable place to sit where you can focus on your breath. Your head should be resting about an inch above the back of the chair or couch you are sitting on. Ensure there are no distractions or anything in the way that could cause you to get distracted from your breathing. Next, sit comfortably with both feet on the ground; this will help you relax as it puts your body in a comfortable position. Then close your eyes and take four deep breaths, making each one deeper than the previous one. Then picture yourself in a place that you find relaxing. This could be your bed, couch, bathtub, or any other place that feels safe to you.

The next step is to focus on how it would feel if you were there. Imagine the smells, sounds, and feel of touch of this place. Think about what it would feel like if you were there; how does it smell? What does the sun feel like when it shines on your face? Is there a breeze? What does it feel like when you are in the water?

These questions are only examples of what you can think about. You can also ask yourself what it would be like to have a conversation with someone or what it would be like to be able to do something. If you feel strange, you can open your eyes and try again later. This is a good exercise because you can focus on the positive instead of trying to figure out everything that is making you anxious at once.

Regular meditation practice will be presented along with five different ways in which adolescents can introduce themselves into their everyday life: journaling, yoga, laughter yoga, massage therapy, and art therapy. For these exercises to work their best, they must be done regularly. The best time would be when there are little or no distractions around you, such as your bedroom, bathroom, or other places where you have time alone. Your mind will focus on these things that are positive and calming, which will help you to feel calm, relaxed, and focused on what you want to achieve. A sense of calmness will come over the individual from practicing meditation regularly, leading to self-awareness and personal growth through reflection induced by one's experiences.

The following are some of the major meditation exercises

Journaling

Journaling is used to become more aware of the things happening around you. A journal can be used for writing about a goal, a problem, or just about the things that happen around you. For example, when you write about your goals, it makes you conceive how far you have come in reaching them and always puts yourself in the right direction to reach them eventually. Journals are an excellent way to help people who might be shy or socially anxious. People with social anxiety may struggle with going up and talking to someone they don't know, but they would much rather write down their thoughts and feelings on a piece of paper than say them out loud. Journaling is an excellent tool for shy people, and it is something they can do by themselves. It can be done in many different ways, with a computer, pencil, paper, or even a tablet. Yoga is another great exercise to practice while journaling.

Yoga

Yoga is an exercise that has been around for thousands of years now. Yoga helps your breathing with different breathing techniques, such as belly breathing. Yogic exercises help you become more aware of your body and muscles, which will help you become more flexible and relax better. Yoga can also be a great exercise to help people who have social anxiety. For example, if you are supposed to give a speech or a presentation, it can help you become more ready for the event because of your body's flexibility.

Laughter Yoga

Laughter Yoga is different from yoga because it focuses on laughing at yourself and everything else around you. Laughter Yoga is used to create joy and make others happy while they are doing it. One great exercise that can be done in this type of class is meditation. A meditation routine could include belly breathing, awareness of your surroundings, and even other people's faces while laughing. Laughter Yoga is great because it works on relaxation and focuses while also enhancing the human spirit and our overall sense of well-being.

Massage Therapy

Massage therapy is an exercise to assist with pain and release tension in your muscles. It can assist with anxiety or any issues causing pain or symptoms (Philadelphia 2012). This exercise can help people with social anxiety because massage can release tension in the body. Massage therapy is a great way for people to relax, allowing them to think more clearly and have a clearer head when they need to make important decisions in their life.

Art Therapy

Art Therapy is an exercise that helps to open up the mind and keeps the individual focused on their goals, values, and beliefs. Art therapy creates a safe place for people to express themselves and explore their thoughts. In art therapy, the individual will take pictures from life or draw pictures from imagination. They are encouraged to spill out their feelings, thoughts, judgments, and perceptions about certain events or issues. Art therapy is great for helping people who are not very social because it allows them to voice their concerns in a way they can understand. The exercise also allows people to think about things differently through a different perspective they may have previously not realized. Art therapy can be used in many different ways, in a classroom setting or even as a part of a little experiment done with a partner.

Many people experience social anxiety attacks when there is an introduction to new people or unfamiliar situations. This type of attack can produce feelings of being nervous, shaking, and feeling like it is difficult to speak. The surge of nervousness in the body from experiencing an attack can cause the person to feel embarrassed and fearful of having another attack in the future. Social anxiety disorder is a psychological disorder that improves over time and through various treatment approaches (Spitzer & Endicott 2004). To treat social anxiety, you will have to educate yourself on the causes and symptoms associated with the disorder. The first step in treating social anxiety is understanding the causes of social anxiety attacks and how they are produced. The second step in treatment is to create a plan that addresses your concern and problem.

The most common causes of social anxiety attacks are limited knowledge or experience with meeting new people, fear or apprehension before an event, unrealistic fears about one's abilities, or being judged negatively by others. When people begin to feel nervous, social anxiety attacks will increase. Statistics show that a higher percentage of humans feel anxious about being in large groups than those who do not. A person with social anxiety disorder typically experiences fear, panic, and worry about scrutiny from others. The individual will experience sweating, rapid heartbeat, and nausea when this occurs. To treat these symptoms, individuals with social anxiety disorder are encouraged to seek help from their doctor or psychiatrist. The therapist will determine the likelihood of a person developing an anxiety disorder and treat them accordingly

Social anxiety disorder is a mental health issue that a psychotherapist and psychologist can treat. Social anxiety is associated with major issues such as depression, general anxiety, phobias, eating disorders, and other mental disorders. People experiencing these issues usually have low self-esteem and perceive themselves to be inadequate in the eyes of others. These individuals experience stress can be debilitating and negatively affect their daily lifestyle (Spitzer & Endicott 2004).

Social anxiety management depends on the unique factors affecting the client. There are many treatment strategies available such as cognitive-behavioral therapy. However, the best way to treat social anxiety disorders is to develop a specific and effective action plan for the individual. An action plan will be created based on what types of thoughts and beliefs you have about yourself, your life, and your relationships with other people. With this information, you can work through exactly what you are feeling and what could be causing these feelings (Spitzer & Endicott, 2004).

Social Anxiety Disorder is treated with one or more of the following interventions: medication, psychotherapy, and other forms of support. Several treatment methods can be used to help manage the symptoms and prevent further episodes from occurring. Therapy can be prescribed by a doctor, psychotherapist, or psychologist.

Cognitive-behavioral therapy is an effective treatment method that helps deal with the cognitive issues associated with anxiety disorders like social anxiety. This therapy works by having patients learn new ways to respond to negative situations that may cause anxiety and worry about what others think about them.

Everyone has different ways of dealing with stress and anxiety; each can work differently for everyone. Some people like to distract themselves with a hobby or a television show, while others prefer to take their minds off things by exercising or meditating.

Having a bad memory or trouble sleeping can be extremely frustrating. Doing something that keeps you distracted for part of the day will help you avoid being on your worst behavior during the night when you are thinking about all your stress. It would be best if you also thought of ways to improve your memory and have a better sleep schedule so that you do not have to struggle through your day anymore. You need to take care of yourself, so you do not feel like there is nothing more you can do. Still, incorporating some proper treatments and exercises into your daily routine will make you feel much better each day.

One of the main things people with anxiety forget is how important they are, and they keep getting caught up in their thoughts, forgetting how great they are. By taking a moment every day to remind yourself of these things and clearing your mind, you will be able to improve your memory and sleep schedule so that they are much easier. I hope that this book has helped to give you some clarity on some of the many issues that you may have been dealing with daily. I hope you now understand how important it is to care for yourself to feel better and stay happy.

Conclusion

After reading this book, you should know better how to improve your relationships with others and yourself. It is important to remember that every person has problems and anxiety at times, but with support and time, you can get through them, so it is important not to beat yourself up when you feel like you are unable to deal with something.

Adolescence is when people learn who they are and what they want in life – but it can also be when they feel confused, unconfident, and anxious about their future. It is important to remember that our bodies, minds, and emotions are connected. The physical structure of our minds depends on the structure of our brains, which give us our emotions and reactions to daily life situations, which affect how we think and feel.

The same can be said for anxiety disorders, as they are caused by genes affecting how we react to stress and emotion. This is then expressed as a physical symptom known as anxiety, which can be corrected similarly. By learning to think positively and act calmly, you will make yourself more confident and relaxed, which can help your relationships and make life easier for everyone involved. It is important to remember that our emotions are caused by what we think and feel before, during, and after a situation. This is not always the case, but it is a good idea to know the facts behind anxiety to ensure that being anxious does not affect your behavior or actions.

It would be best if you also remembered that learning the techniques in this booklet will go hand in hand with any therapy that your doctor or other professionals prescribe. It is important to remember that you should always try to do things for yourself instead of waiting for others to do them for you. You should also talk about your problems with people close to you, such as family or friends, so that if your anxiety does not get any better, you or those around you can be helped further.

You will find that as long as you continue to do the exercises in this book for some time, your anxiety will become less severe and, at some point, disappear.

I hope that reading this book has helped you to feel better about your problems and has given you the confidence to help yourself and others.

This book is aimed at helping teenagers who are going through anxiety and depression because as adolescents explore their thoughts, feelings, and emotions for the first time in their lives, it is important that they feel confident about themselves and happy with what they are doing. With the help of this book, you should be able to deal with your problems better from now on!

I hope you have learned how your mind works and how it affects your daily life. I also hope you can control your negative thoughts and choose to think positively about yourself instead.

For this to work, remember that everything you do is important for your future. You are only limited by the amount of time you have, so if you have a goal that you want to achieve, then focus on that and reach your goal no matter how hard it may be!

By choosing to succeed and going through all the hard work, you will naturally feel better about yourself, and people will start to like and respect you for who you are.

I hope this book has assisted in giving you some clarity and has helped your life to become more positive.

Finally, I hope that you will be able to understand that you are a great person and that you are already capable of achieving whatever you set your mind to, so why not give it a go?!

You must read it again and keep it so you can refer back to it when necessary. If you have others suffering from anxiety, share this with them so they will understand more about what you are going through.

Be patient with yourself, and remember that practice makes perfect! When the thoughts start to cloud your mind, you must replace them with another thought or activity. Make sure you do this as often as possible to help your brain adjust and start training itself to use the same pathways every time a new thought comes into your head.

Printed in Great Britain
by Amazon